PEEKING THROUGH BLIND JUSTICE

ONE PERSON'S FIGHT AGAINST *Workplace Discrimination*

MARCY RICH

outskirts press

I dedicate this book to my two wonderful daughters and my two fabulous sons-in-law.

I especially dedicate this book to my grandchildren-born and soon to be born. This is Bubbe's legacy to you and a reminder to always be a Mensch.

Acknowledgements

Special thanks goes out to my family, friends, associates and 3 super co-workers who were extremely supportive during the 3 years that my lawsuit was alive.

Thank you to the numerous other authors who gave me great suggestions for marketing and promoting my book.

Thank you to all those who had a part in making this book possible:

- Michael Murriett of Social Secret Agent who was a great hand holder during my book writing process

- Alexander Krivitskiy for his photograph used on the front cover

- Tolga Tuncay of Hollywood Photo Studios for my headshot photo

- The defense in the lawsuit-both the company and their attorney

- Every educator and mentor who taught me the strategies we can all use to be better human beings

A very special thanks goes out to my parents whom I never got a chance to thank for making me realize how important it is to be a Mensch.

Table of Contents

Introduction

When I first met my attorney, I told him I was filing a lawsuit because I am an American and a Jew. As an American, I am responsible for advising of unlawful discrimination. As a Jew, I am obligated to uphold, "NEVER AGAIN."

During my tenure as a high school English teacher, the original miniseries Roots made its debut. Fifteen months later the miniseries, Holocaust, was initially aired. During that week an African American student of mine walked into the classroom, shook my hand, and acknowledged the mutual understanding we now have of each other. Fast forward to present time.

My case, the foundation of this book, is my own version of

Black Lives Matter  and  movements.

I tossed and turned about writing this book and yet every time a 'nay' came through, 5 'yeas' overrode it. I continually was prompted by many who told me, "you have a message-you need to make it global."

While working on the book I read and reread all the documents and depositions associated with my lawsuit. I noticed many inaccuracies. Defense told falsehoods, manipulated data, and worse of all, defamed my character all in public records open to anyone. I feel it is my responsibility to myself and to my family to let the truth be known since lies should never be allowed to exist as if they were true. I cannot in any way justify having lies about me and my character go undisputed. If defense wanted to lie to the Federal Court, it is their prerogative. I choose the truth.

Because Summary Judgment did not go in my favor, I was not able to tell my story in court. I figured if I couldn't tell my story to a jury of 12, I would tell my story to a world of 7 billion.

One thing about being embroiled in litigation with the company for which you work-you get to see their flaws through a clearer lens. I decided to take what I learned from their mistakes, couple it with my knowledge of organizational development and experience in relation-ship coaching, and help others do the right thing the right way. When people and organizations work this way, they are being a Mensch * (a person of integrity and honor. The term is used as a high compliment, implying the rarity and value of that individual's qualities-a person with the qualities one would hope for in a friend or trusted colleague).

This book is about being a Mensch-in life and in the work place. It is about treating others with respect and dignity. It is time for each of us to choose being a Mensch and for all organizations, companies, and corporations to make this a part of their business as usual.

As a 'specialist in the people side of life' (self-proclamation), my life purpose is to help others- companies as a whole and people individu-ally- always attest to being a Mensch in their actions and words. One by one, as each human reaches this level we can start to rid the world of indifference and insensitivity.

I am not an attorney and am not educated in law so am not offering any legal advice. The legal information presented in this book is from my perception and point of view of my experience although most is taken verbatim from public court records and everything is factual. Please use my information only as a launching pad to do much more research.

I am though well-educated and experienced in organizational design and human behavior and am offering proven methods and strategies for better interactions.

My purpose is to share with others what I have learned not only from my lawsuit but from my work and life experiences, daily studies, and academia in hopes of helping, healing and harmonizing so we have a world of Mensches.

It is about every human being-being human.

The Company named in the lawsuit gave me an abundance of material to use to help other companies who strive to loosen their reins on having an ego driven leadership. In this book I use the issues presented in my EEOC charge and lawsuit complaint to show how organizations-and people- can all fall into the category of Mensch doing the right thing-and doing it the right way. The lack of humanity and compassion are not good drivers of an organization or for any individual. Using the lawsuit as a basis of discussion, I hope every organization can become humane and compassionate and every leader can be a Mensch.

My intention for writing this book is not to call anyone out. For that reason I am not using the company name. To identify them I use the terms: company, organization, or defendant. Rather than use individual names I use either initials or job title.

The contents of this book are ideal for (but not limited to)
- Leaders in organizations and in life
- Human Resource Staff members
- Lawyers and law students

- People who don't like bigotry and prejudice

- People who do like bigotry and prejudice and need to know
  why neither is good

- Each of you who has something to say and haven't yet listened
  to your quiet wise inner voice that encourages you to access
  your courageous self and speak for your beliefs.

The book is divided into 3 parts:
1. <u>The legal process</u>-takes you through filing with EEOC to
   choosing an attorney to filing a complaint all the way through
   Summary Judgment and the Judge's final ruling
2. <u>Diversity and religion</u>-talks about how our differences need to
   be acknowledged and not judged
3. <u>Organizations</u>-describing actions and techniques to change
   an organization from a non-Mensch culture to a Mensch
   culture

Soon after the Summary Judgment was granted to defense by the
Judge, I met with an attorney, who had no affiliation with my case,
to discuss some items now that the case was over. He said to me, "I
don't know why your employer chose winning over settling so you
would have a gag order. So, go ahead now and write your book!"

> **"Sometimes stories cry out to be told in such loud
> voices that you write them just to shut them up."**
>
> –Stephen King

This is my story that is crying to be told.

*Per <u>Leo Rosten</u>, author of <u>*The Joys of Yiddish*</u>, a "*mensch*" is „someone to admire and emulate, someone of noble character. The key to
being ‚a real mensch' is nothing less than character, rectitude, dignity,
and a sense of what is right.

Part 1
The Legal Process

CHAPTER 1

Making the Decision

I GREW UP on the south side of Chicago in a neighborhood called South Shore. At that time the area was 100% white with a strong population of Jews. Often times my family would drive down the street that held a building labeled, "South Shore Country Club." No one in my family ever mentioned it and my friends and I never spoke about it. It was as if it were invisible-just a mirage in the big city. In my late teen years I learned that it was an exclusive club outwardly banning Jews. Signs inside were reputed to declare in some form, "No Jews allowed." I learned it was not just the Jews but the African-Americans as well who were unwelcome.

Many years later at the end of a class I was instructing, an African-American class participant engaged in a conversation with me. He told me he also lived in South Shore, albeit a couple of decades after I moved from there. South Shore Country Club became our focus of discussion as we both were victims of its bigotry.

He told me he and his friends were determined that this blatant exclusion would not go untouched so one night they "jumped the wall and went inside." "Good for you," I said. "We (the Jews) should have done the same thing."

In February of 2013 I determined it was time for me to 'jump the wall' that screams discrimination.

It is a big step to file a discrimination charge-especially when still working for the company. I did not take this decision lightly. I repeatedly told both CEO's under whose auspices I worked, about my dissatisfaction with my staying stagnant in my position. When I reached the point of no return, when I witnessed that the second CEO, CM, perpetuated the open and blatant discriminatory behavior of his direct predecessor by promoting others, giving others different positions and titles, and always bypassing me, I knew this was the culture and philosophy of the organization. Connecting the dots was easy now. I was well qualified and educated, proven to be an exemplary employee, had extensive longevity with the organization, and was well liked and praised by our subscribers as well as my peers. I was also the only Jew ever employed in the organization.

I did my research about Title VII, the federal law stating:

Title VII of the Civil Rights Act of 1964 is a federal law that protects employees against discrimination based on certain specified characteristics: race, color, national origin, sex, and religion. Under Title VII, an employer may not discriminate with regard to any term, condition, or privilege of employment. Areas that may give rise to violations include recruiting, hiring, promoting, transferring, training, disciplining, discharging, assigning work, measuring performance, or providing benefits. No person ...can be denied employment or treated differently with regard to any workplace decision on the basis of perceived racial, religious, national, sexual, or religious characteristics.

In its simplicity, it is rather misleading and misrepresenting. I took it literally that no employer may discriminate in promoting employees. I was blinded by the huge gap between the written statement of the law and the implementation of it.

To show discrimination in the workplace is anything but black and white, I am presenting very specific information about EEOC and the legal process-as I experienced it.

Having established a support system consisting of my two sisters, two daughters, and two co-workers, I was ready to move forward and my final words to the CEO, CM, before I went to file my complaint was, "I will need to do what I need to do." He seemed to respond favorably making me perceive his action as believing I would leave the company.

The law requires that a complaint be first filed with the Title VII enforcement agency, such as EEOC (Equal Employment Opportunity Commission) before filing a lawsuit. This requirement is in place to remedy the situation early on and eliminate the need to go to court.

Having not done this before or known anyone who had, I was a bit green about protocol. I wrote a 5 page document about my grievance. Even if the EEOC did not need all that information, I knew it would still be advantageous for me to have it written up for future reference.

I was right. This 5 page document, while not initially sent to the defendant, was attached to the EEOC Intake Questionnaire and available for review later by the defendant.

Some of the items I stated in this document were instrumental in my classifying the company's actions as discriminatory.

- The CEO (RB) filled a new position, Support Services Manager, with an outside candidate despite his telling staff that "everything being equal, an internal candidate would be offered positions in the organization." I was 100% skilled, experienced, and educated for this position so was shocked when I was rejected. I asked him for clarification as to why I was not the selected candidate by referencing his stated commitment to promote within when everything is equal. He told me he did not see it as equal to which I replied, "ok, let's start with the obvious-I have a master's degree in organizational development with a concentration in training and development, I was a H.S. English teacher, and did training for a fortune 100 company. She has a H.S. diploma. Where are we equal?"

No response from him.

- I was denied another new position for which this same CEO said I was qualified. Then he abruptly changed his mind and placed an outside candidate in the position. All other manager positions were filled internally and usually by someone already in the respected department.

- The person who got the Support Services Manager position (HB) had her title immediately upgraded to Support Services Director making her in charge of both the training and support departments. I asked the CEO (RB) to split the department and give HB the support department and give me the training department. His laughter was followed by his unequivocal refusal to do such.

Yet shortly thereafter, CM came on board and RB did indeed split the Support Services and gave CM the support department and left the training department to HB. By this time HB was in her role of Support Services Director for 5 years and proved way too many times she was not the right person for it. I was still denied the position.

- Once CM replaced the resigned RB as CEO, I met with him on 6 occasions hoping he would reverse the wrong prejudicial overt actions inflicted on me in the recent past regarding changing my job role and function. In our discussions I gave him every opportunity to change the culture of the organization from prejudiced to tolerant and open. He indicated to me both overtly and covertly that he was not going to do so. My being bypassed for promotions or change of job title continued.

- When I asked CM to rightfully and deservedly promote me, he said there were no vacancies and "we already have too many managers." Yet he created several vacancies filled by other staff members as well as new candidates.

- In the last meeting I had with CM, I asked that he trade out the current training manager, HB, with me. By this time it was common knowledge that she was completely inept and incompetent in doing her job. Again he refused to do so saying, "I am not willing to do that…I am capable but not willing." He allegedly told an exiting employee that he knew HB was the wrong person for the position.

All of these items grabbed hold of me intellectually and I knew there was only one place to go…

CHAPTER 2

It all begins with EEOC

The waiting room

WITH THE 5 page document in hand along with the intake questionnaire form required by the EEOC, I went to the Phoenix office in February 2013 to start what turned out to be a long, often times frustrating, many times exhausting endeavor. It was also a forever life changing, learning and rewarding experience for me.

I was in the waiting room with two other individuals who came empty handed and filled out the form as they sat waiting. One was an African-American woman who stated she did not get a job because she was Black, and the other was a man who said he was terminated from his job for using Marijuana even though he had a medical Marijuana card.

I was now convinced I had a case.

Meeting with the agent

I was assigned to the EEOC agent, *OG*, who told me he read through my grievance on why this case qualifies as discrimination. He proceeded to ask me clarifying questions. Using both my statement along with the intake questionnaire I filled out and my verbal statements, he wrote up a summation on the EEOC official 'Charge of Discrimination' form using me as the writer. My 2951+ words were reduced to 293. While his summation made clear I asked for promotions or a different position and mentioned "I believe I have been the victim of unlawful employment practices due to my religion (Jewish) in violation of Title VII of the Civil Rights Act of 1964 as amended," the summation unfortunately did not seem to capture the essence of anti-Semitism and hence discrimination as a key factor.

The EEOC agent suggested we don't attach my written claim. I trusted his expertise in advising me 'less is more' and other than my correcting a couple of misstatements he made and a couple of typos or grammatical errors, I accepted what he wrote. I signed it, thanked him, and walked out of the office.

I immediately called my sister and with elation and joy, elicited proudly, "I did it!" My first step of this journey was accomplished.

Defense gets notified

The CEO of the organization received 3 pages from EEOC a few days after my meeting with them letting him know of the claim. One page is referenced as the Notice of Charge of Discrimination and the other two pages were the Charge which included the 5 small paragraphs succinctly stating the issue.

Timelines exist in the world of EEOC

- The Notice of Charge of Discrimination advised defense they had up until a certain date to provide a statement of their position and any documentation to support it. This information would be put into the file and considered in EEOC's investigation.

- Once I received a copy of the defense's statement after I formally requested it (mandated by EEOC), I was given 21 days to respond. I was informed that if I failed to respond within that time period, "the Commission will have no choice but to base its investigation on the information contained in the case file." EEOC received via email and fax my rebuttal within 17 days. The rebuttal was filed with the case but not shared (at that time-important to know) with defense.

- Per law, the incident that prompted the cause to file must have been no more than 300 days prior. Since most incidences are not always so blatant in the moment, it is hard to determine when they occurred. The issues that showed discrimination in my case were most visible through the rear-view mirror.

My submitted documentation covered this when I stated, "…I realize now I have been a victim of unlawful employment practices enduring much discriminatory conduct directed at me that has been continuous and ongoing. While I suspected many behaviors, events, decisions and incidences to be prejudicial, I either tried to find other excuses or thought each individually may have been insignificant for major action."

In the section of The Charge of Discrimination form asking for *Date(s) Discrimination Took Place*, the *Earliest* date was left blank and the *Latest* date indicated the same month of my filing the claim. I placed an 'X' in the box stating *Continuing Action*.

Nonetheless, defense continually used the 'time barred' card to get the case dismissed-both with the EEOC and later with the Federal Court.

This is worthy to note: There is no box to check stating *hostile work environment*.

- The employer is afforded the opportunity, clearly stated on the Notice of Charge of Discrimination, to participate in mediation (no cost) to settle the situation without further action of EEOC or Federal Court-an action highly advocated by both government institutions. The notice gives the name and phone number of the ADR (Alternative Dispute Resolution) coordinator and a date by which this person must be contacted to schedule a meeting. This date comes before the date required for the Position Statement in hopes of making such unnecessary. In spite of the defense attorney claiming they were making "an attempt to expedite the EEOC's investigation in this matter," my employer refused mediation and opted for hiring an attorney and prolonging the whole process. In other words, they chose to proverbially make a 'federal case' out of this. I, on the other hand, informed the EEOC agent with whom I met that I would be open to mediation.

The learning part of my experience continued on as I read through the response defense submitted. I learned all about 'prima facie' – the responsibility of the plaintiff to present sufficient evidence to support the legal claim. With sufficient evidence, discrimination is presumed. In such a situation, the defense would need to rebut the evidence presented with a legitimate, non-discriminating reason for its employment decision. The plaintiff would then be able to attempt proving the legitimate reason given was only a cover for discrimination.

Without sufficient evidence from the plaintiff, defense could request a dismissal of the case. It is this route that defense took in their response.

I also learned the defense attorney was capable of twisting what I said, inferring meaning that was inaccurate, and relying on erroneous information received from his client. It was just the start of his doing such.

In his response, defense attorney stated I claimed I should "have been offered a part time HR position to assist in payroll processing." He continues to state I considered the job should have gone to me and I should have been selected over the other candidate. Nothing could be further from the truth. I never asked to have that position. I never wanted to be considered for that position. I never would have. What I requested the CEO do was to split the HR function into two: one side to work compensation and benefits – keeping the current HR person in place who was outstanding in her performance as such and the other to work staff development/employee relations where I could perform excellently per my education and experience.

My reason for mentioning this episode in my claim was to show that the CEO told me he could not create another position yet he did to establish an assistant to the HR staff member. My claim actually states: "I told him (CEO) I was well qualified in staff development for Employee Relations, but it was refused…I also suggested taking on a position of staff development due to my experience in that area and (was) told that managers were not ready for it, yet the managers were sent to Florida for management training." There is nothing in my claim even suggesting I asked the CEO to give me the position of assistant to HR staff member. Therefore, I agree 100% with the position statement: "there is no basis to suggest Ms. Rich was discriminated against because of her religion by not being offered the part-time HR position."

My claim also states: "I asked to be removed from reporting to that position (education manager) and (was) denied. However, non-Jewish individuals…asked to be removed from reporting to their managers and it (request) was approved."

In response to this part of my claim, defense wrote I was requesting "(she) should be allowed to report to someone other than her current supervisor…because non-Jewish employees have been able to switch supervisors if they did not like reporting to their current supervisor."

His use of the word *because* leads one to believe I was seeing this issue as a cause and effect. Again, nothing is further from the truth. I was proving that when a non-Jewish person requested it, the request was granted. I was not afforded the consideration. *Treating similarly situated employees…more favorably* is a main component of discrimination.

Defense did request in his response that I "identify the alleged similarly situated employees who were allegedly treated differently." In my rebuttal, I addressed this by naming names and situations.

Defense clearly took a great deal of liberties. Apparently he was practicing for Summary Judgment (to be discussed later).

Finally, defense asked the EEOC to dismiss the Charge with a 'No Cause' finding.

Continuing on with EEOC

The four main ingredients needed for the investigation to move forward were now in place:

- Claim had been submitted and filed with EEOC

- Claim had been presented to the company

- Position statement had been received and filed by EEOC

- Claimant' rebuttal to position statement had been received and filed by EEOC

Now it was a matter of waiting for the investigation to start rolling. While my investigator at EEOC advised me the investigation actually starts at the moment the claim is filed, it can stay dormant for quite some time. To do my part in keeping it active and hopefully forefront, I kept EEOC apprised of anything that added substantiation to my claim. The next step was to show claims of retaliation.

- August, 2013: I sent my EEOC agent an email stating the company was beginning to set a paper trail illustrating retaliatory behavior. The company received an anonymous typed letter allegedly from a person who was in my class making negative comments about me. The letter, having no signature other than 'anonymous' and having no letterhead, no return address, no date, and no indication of what class, date or time of the incidence made me consider this letter very questionable. The content of the letter was full of absurdities including false accusations, erroneous information and unsubstantiated data. There was no evidence from feedback surveys filled out by class members that anyone was dismayed by any of my instructed classes. Nevertheless, the Director of my department proceeded to give it to the HR person to file in my personnel folder prior to even talking to me about it and without scrutinizing the information contained.

Because there was no evidence this letter was from a class participant and no evidence it was NOT from someone inside the company setting me up, it was worth my submitting it to include in my EEOC file in the event it may prove beneficial down the road. I was prepared.

- October 2013: Another incident occurred that indicated retaliatory behavior so again I sent my findings in an email to the EEOC agent. This time my manager gave me my first "unacceptable" on my quarterly review. She provided no concrete evidence for her decision making it a very subjective evaluation. It helped solidify my contention that I was treated differently than others in the same situation who were outside my protected class. Two of my team members admitted having the same situation occur for them yet were not penalized by having an "unacceptable" rating in any category on their review.

Ending with EEOC

It is mandated that claimants filing with EEOC about discrimination allow the agency 180 days to investigate and resolve the charge. When doing so, the claimant is taking on their responsibility to 'exhaust administrative remedies.' Per the literature I read about claims with EEOC, many are resolved within this time period.

After approximately 140 days into my case, I asked my agent for a status update. He let me know he did not have any specifics on a timeframe for going forward because he was working on priority cases and older cases. Then 3 months later there was a government shutdown. I was sure the shutdown would not help my case's ranking as a priority.

My intent had always been to resolve this issue early on but with the EEOC not moving forward on this and my company not making any attempt to discuss this with me, I decided to go another path after I determined a couple of profound reasons to move my case from agency to attorney.

- There is a maximum allotted for compensatory and punitive damages with EEOC whereas there is not this same limit through federal court.

- Working with an attorney would make me a client rather than a case number.

Word to the wise if you are preparing to file a charge

- If you have filed and want to add more information, be sure to amend it or make a whole new charge. What is written in the charge with EEOC is imperative and is the foundation of a complaint (lawsuit). I was sure I did this when I added the retaliation items. I emailed the agent at EEOC twice asking him if the company gets a copy of the added items I included in the charge and he left me a voice message which has long been erased and forgotten. I know I felt secure that he was doing what was required. I am advising this because defense repeatedly reported not been given notice on many items in my charge.

- Work with an attorney while filing charge. I am not questioning the ability or professionalism of the EEOC agent. The agency is inundated with charges-some valid, many not. They have the responsibility of looking over each situation. No doubt, this can be stressful, time consuming, and demanding. Also, there is virtually no relationship that is nurtured during the investigation. Filing a charge with the EEOC simply puts the agency on alert that there may be a violation of Title VII and an investigation may be needed to ascertain if indeed there is. They may simplify their statements to reduce complexity in doing their job.

- Be sure the statement you sign with the EEOC is complete-in fact, more than complete. Yes, leave room for flexibility but not so much that too many corners are cut. What I could have done differently was to summarize my 5 page report so that we attach it to the EEOC form delineating the charge. If I had done so, defense would not have been able to claim in their Motion to Dismiss that the first time the company learned that I was subjected to a hostile work environment was when it was served with the complaint.

- Be sure to use the word, 'discrimination' to the company and be sure to show every incident is tied to your protected class. This shows a causal link which is important for the case. I should not have assumed that my comments to the HR Director or the CEO of the company indicated I was claiming discrimination. I would have done well if I had asked, "Are you not promoting me because I am Jewish? I feel this is the reason." Follow any formality the company expects when telling them your concerns. Be sure you get a response from them in writing.

- Make the documents you submit initially to EEOC available to the company. At the very least, be sure you summarize enough that the essence of everything in your charge is available to the other party.

I began the second part of my journey in October 2013-seeking an attorney to represent me.

CHAPTER 3

Starting the lawsuit

Choosing the attorney: To pay or not to pay

IN THIS DAY of technology it is not so difficult to find an attorney-just hard to find one that you feel will take your case and work to a good conclusion. I interviewed several lawyers-none of whom said I did not have a case; none of whom said I did have a case. Most told me what happens in a discrimination case and only one asked me more and more questions letting me know that by scouring and scrubbing, he would retrieve the information from me he needed. He also told me my case would probably incur a minimum of $40,000 in attorney fees. And of course that comes with no guarantee of a win. I continued my internet search and found another major law firm who via phone and within minutes told me they would take my case-and if that weren't enough, they worked on a contingency basis. They get paid if I get paid; albeit they receive 40%. This amount could add up to much more than the $40,000 the other attorney quoted me but at least I would not be out any money if I did not win. The answer for me was easy-go with paying the 40%. At the beginning of November 2013, I signed a contract with them.

I was assigned to one of the four attorneys who work in this segment of the firm. The managing partner told me the attorney assigned to me would be assisting me on the day to day aspects of my case and he would be overseeing their work. It was the latter statement of his that kept me staying with the firm.

I had reservations about the attorney to whom I was first assigned.

Some of her behaviors caused my concern about using an attorney that worked on contingency.

- She missed meetings with me.

- She seemed to consciously let me know how much work she was putting in on my case with comments such as (regarding writing up the initial complaint) "I spent a considerable amount of time today review[sic] the EEOC document you sent, as well as your comments in the complaint." Regarding responding to Defendant's Motion to Dismiss: "Our time needs to be spent reading court opinions and a lot of time spent drafting and redrafting argument to make the best response possible for the judge."

- She encouraged me to drop the case. Her reasoning was

  » My case may not show enough pervasive actions by the company

  » I would probably need to pay defendant's attorney fees if I lose

I was determined to go forward with my case-win or lose. I had something to say and I had plenty of skin in the game this far. I was not letting it go. The attorney was going to meet with the managing partner to discuss this and get back with me. The next day I heard back from her and she told me that in a Title VII case, if the plaintiff loses, defense cannot get their fees paid unless it is found that the plaintiff's action was frivolous, unreasonable, or without foundation. Of course it concerned me that she did not know this originally. We both knew my case did not fall into any of those categories. In that same conversation she talked about the issue of pervasive behavior. She proceeded to ask me if a swastika would be offensive to a Jew. Knowing she wasn't sure about something so obvious, I was thoroughly convinced of the importance of my continuing on with my case. There was more work for me to do as an American and as a Jew.

Needless to say, I was not upset when I learned in September 2014 she was no longer a part of the firm.

I was also delighted that I was assigned now to the attorney and paralegal who had taken my case temporarily earlier that year. From that time on, I was treated extremely well. All my emails and calls were answered timely and my issues were always addressed kindly and accurately.

The question if one should pay the attorney by the hour or work on contingency has no clear cut answer. For me, the only way to go was to work on contingency. My first thought when told this was the law firm's business model was that they would work very hard to win since that would be the only way they would get paid. While that theory has merit, it is also conceivable that at some point they cut their losses using a cost/benefit analysis. Was it worth their work, time, and effort to continue? After all, going to trial is extremely expensive with no guarantees for either side. To be clear, I thought my attorneys worked hard on my case and went into it full force. I also thought there was a time they may have considered abandoning ship was in the firm's best interest. On the other hand, I didn't owe them any money and good chance even if I did use an attorney who charged by the hour, I would still not have won and would have been out the money.

Writing the complaint

Our first action was to advise the EEOC I was now being legally represented and to request a 'right to sue' letter from the agency. I received this letter on 12/3/13 –an instrumental date in the process because it begins the 90 day maximum requirement to file a lawsuit in federal court. After 90 days, the court will not accept the complaint. Time was of the essence.

Writing up the complaint was our next action. This took quite some time. On January 3, 2014, my attorney's assistant told me they were currently working on my complaint. After several rewrites and edits to verify actual details alleged, to remove inaccuracies and to complete anything that was incomplete, the complaint was filed on February 5, 2014.

The Arizona Corporation Commission, the entity of record to receive legal papers for the defense, was served the summons on February 19, 2014. They would send the document to the company. I was now officially a Federal Case assigned Case Number: 2:14-CV-00213-JWS. The last three letters indicate the Judge assigned to the case.

This was one of those rewarding moments about which I spoke earlier even though it took some time for me to totally comprehend the magnitude of what I just accomplished. I filed a lawsuit in Federal Court!

A religious discrimination case needs to meet 4 criteria:

- The plaintiff must belong to a protected class (Jewish is considered a protected class)

- The plaintiff was performing her job in a satisfactory manner

- The plaintiff suffered an adverse employment action

- Similarly situated employees outside of her protected class were treated more favorably

To show I was treated differently than others in the organization because of my religion, to show I was discriminated against in being promoted, and to show there was a religiously hostile work environment created, the complaint pointed out some of the following:

- My direct supervisor, a born-again Christian told me I was 'dead' because I did not reveal Jesus to me.

- A company mandated holiday party not only had a Cross on the invitation but also employed 'carolers' who sang religious songs with lyrics "Christ our Lord."

- I was repeatedly interrogated as to why I preferred they give their gift of a Poinsettia at Christmas time to one of my co-workers. I was not comfortable having it since it is a Christmas plant, a holiday which is not in line with my Jewish faith.

- My manager sent an email to department members wishing everyone a happy holiday no matter if they "celebrate the birth of Christ or the Chanukah candles"

- Positions were created and/or populated with employees less qualified than I (per area of expertise) routinely even though I had clearly voiced my interest in other positions and other roles. I was always told in some way, "No."

- I met with the CEO (had role of COO at some of the meetings) on at least 6 different occasions to discuss the religiously hostile culture and constant thrust of Christian religion and ideology upon me. To my knowledge he never investigated claims.

- I was retaliated against after I filed with EEOC by being denied advancement and being subjected to a more rigorous and arbitrary standard of performance evaluation not used with other employees.

I was now on a journey of learning how the legal system works. Here are some quick 'take-a-ways' from my experience-some of what I already knew but were punctuated in the circuitous route of law.

- Winning a case takes one argument to be better than the other

- Even case studies can have different interpretations

- Each side can find cases that back up their argument and disregard cases that don't.

I always consider this last item to be what I call, "the coffee theory." I am a big coffee drinker so I always read articles that say coffee is good for you and I ignore articles that say otherwise.

Once defense was served papers, they had 21 days to respond. Time seemed to be doable-so I thought. On March 17, 2014 my attorney sent me an email stating:

"The defendant did not file an Answer to the complaint. Instead, they filed a Motion to Dismiss. This means we need to file a response to the Motion to Dismiss, and then the judge will decide if your case can continue or not. The Defendant will not need to submit an Answer unless the judge rules in our favor and denies the Motion to Dismiss. The Motion to Dismiss is quite legally complicated, and it can take up to a few months for the issues to be fully briefed by both sides and for a judge to rule on the motion."

She informed me that our response would require quite a bit of legal research and writing to counter the legal arguments made by the Defendant. She approximated it taking up to 4-6 weeks to file our response.

This was my first major setback.

She continued to advise me: "the motion to dismiss argument is solely legal in nature. We cannot allege any additional facts. It comes down to researching court decisions, and us making arguments regarding what the law is in an area to dispute what they say the law is…It will come down to what the law is, and how the circumstances here fit into that law. The judge will end up deciding on whether to grant or reject the motion to dismiss. If he dismisses it, as we ask for, the case will continue on. If the judge grants their motion to dismiss, your case gets dismissed."

Motion to Dismiss

Stated here very succinctly are the issues presented in the Motion to Dismiss, my (plaintiff's) response, and the defendants' reply in support of Motion to Dismiss. I am being specific in this section and many times quoting from the actual court document because:

- I want to be sure I am accurate in what I tell you

- I have no idea how to paraphrase some of these items

The Motion to Dismiss and the Reply in Support of Motion to Dismiss filed by the Defendants focused on a few main areas:

- Claims are time-barred

Defense worked from the premise that events need to take place no more than 300 days from filing a charge with the EEOC. Since my hostile work environment claim is based primarily upon discrete events alleged occurring in December 2011 and the charge was not filed until February 19, 2013, defense stated my claim of hostile work environment was out of the time parameters of 300 days. Only three events alleged fell within 300 days of filing. Additionally, defense stated that my claim that I was not promoted six years prior is time barred-well out of the 300 day time period allotted.

To this, we (plaintiff) provided our response.

The complaint shows the ongoing continuation of the harassment and hostile environment created by members of (company's) management. Sufficient notice to Defendant was given of the underlying basis for the claims.

We cited a case that states "events occurring outside of the limitations period can form the basis of a Title VII claim as long as the untimely incidents represent an ongoing unlawful employment practice…the plaintiff must demonstrate the untimely incidents are part of a pattern of discrimination and that the employer continued this pattern into the relevant limitation's period. The plaintiff would need to present evidence of a series of related discriminatory acts directed at her by the employer's personnel."

Using the 'continuing violation' theory, we argued that discriminatory acts outside of the 300 day window itemized in my complaint are still actionable as constituent parts of my Title VII claims.

Defendant's responded to this in their "Reply to Support Motion to Dismiss."

- The Supreme Court…ruled that the continuing violation theory is applicable only to hostile work environment claims and **_not_** (emphasis in document) disparate treatment and retaliation claims.

- Failure to file a discrimination charge until five years later should be excused under the continuing violation theory

- "A plaintiff cannot create a new cause of action and/or new statute of limitations by asking an employer to take corrective action because she is unhappy that she did not receive a promotion."

Defense applied their argument to show my repeatedly asking the company to correct its prior employment decisions and to promote me does not qualify for the continuing violation theory.

A learning moment for me: The 9th Circuit adopted this reasoning noting that to do otherwise would make it nearly impossible for a charging party to ever have an untimely claim.

As I mentioned earlier, when filing a discrimination charge, one first needs to file with EEOC (or another such agency). Even though I had done so, defense claims I did not exhaust all my administrative remedies.

Defense claimed the charge with EEOC did not address any allegations regarding a hostile work environment. They contend that all the events in my complaint that I used to illustrate the hostile work environment were not in the charge. Per the motion, because hostile work environment was not stated in the charge and the lawsuit can only encompass allegations within the ambit of the EEOC charge and now raised for the first time in the complaint, it should be dismissed (note: allegations regarding hostile work environment came after defense received charge as I mentioned earlier).

Our (plaintiff's) response pointed out the following:

- Causes like or reasonably related to the allegations of the charger (plaintiff) or that grow out of the original charge for discrimination should be entertained. Although I did not check-mark a box for "hostile work environment" (my addition here- there is no such box to checkmark on the charge or intake form) on my EEOC charge, such a claim is reasonably related to and grows out of the original charge of religious discrimination. My claims related to the Defendant's conduct (the company) were examples of the religious hostility that pervaded the company.

- The court must give liberal construction to the EEOC charge as it is often drafted by lay individuals not expert in drafting formal pleadings, and therefore not held to the same strict pleading requirements of a complaint.

- A court's inquiry…should encompass the entire EEOC claim. Because retaliation charges that stem from the EEOC charge are often excepted from the exhaustion requirement, the claim of retaliation cannot be dismissed for failing to exhaust administrative remedies.

In response to defense's statement that I failed to state a claim upon which relief may be granted, my Attorney's research showed that all that is required of the plaintiff is "a short and plain statement of the claim showing that the pleader is entitled to relief…give the defendant fair notice of what the…claim is and the grounds upon which it rests"

Some other arguments worthy of note:

Defense also refuted my claim of working in a hostile work environment. They continued in their motion that my allegations and references to situations that occurred did not involve the extreme type of conduct necessary to establish a hostile work environment claim to alter the terms and conditions of my employment.

Our Response.

An employer is liable under Title VII for conduct giving rise to a hostile environment where the employee proves

- S/he was subjected to verbal or physical conduct of a harassing nature

- This conduct was unwelcome

- The conduct was sufficiently severe or pervasive to alter the conditions of the victim's employment and create an abusive working environment

My response states that I was the target of conduct that was sufficiently offensive and pervasive that objectively one would be offended by the comments and conduct of the Defendant.

The motion continues to assert that because I 'suffered no adverse employment action, [I] had no disparate treatment claim.' Adverse employment action, as detailed in the motion (and Defendant's reply in support of Motion to Dismiss), would include being demoted, getting a decrease in salary or other benefits, being fired or suspended, or being stripped of work responsibilities, being handed more burdensome work responsibilities, or being denied raises.

We countered this.

The Ninth Circuit has held that a denial of promotion qualifies as an adverse employment action. We noted that in February 2013 I asked the CEO to trade out my position with my manager's to which he said he was capable of doing such but not willing to do so.

- Defense attempted to show I did not have a retaliation claim since my more 'rigorous' performance evaluations did not cause a decrease in pay or any other type of cognizable adverse employment action or suffer any other cognizable impact as a result of the evaluation. Additionally I received no discipline as a result. Per their Motion, "The allegation that I was held to a rigorous performance evaluation, without more, fails to state a claim upon which relief may be granted and the claim should be dismissed."

We countered this.

The Ninth Circuit has held that an undeserved negative performance review can constitute an adverse employment decision.

- Finally defense stated that my claim of retaliation should be dismissed because (per the filed Motion to Dismiss) I did not properly allege any causal connection between the alleged retaliatory acts taken against me and my alleged complaints. According to defense, there was not sufficient evidence to raise the interference that my protected activity was the likely reason for the adverse action-no causal link existed between the protected activity and the employment decision.

We responded.

"At this stage in the litigation, the causal link is construed broadly; a plaintiff must merely allege 'that the protected activity and the negative employment action are not completely unrelated.'"

My learning moment: From our response to their Motion to Dismiss, I learned about requesting a leave to amend. In our response my attorneys asked the court that if it found cause to dismiss my complaint that the court would grant a Leave to Amend. The court considers five factors in assessing the propriety of leave to amend. They include:

bad faith, undue delay, prejudice to the opposing party, futility of amendment, and whether the plaintiff had previously amended the complaint. The request continued to delineate how I am good on all five factors.

- None of my claims were alleged in bad faith

- I believe the facts show a prima facie case for each of the claims

- Defendant would not be prejudice by such an amendment as they are represented by counsel and would be given the necessary time to prepare an answer and a defense

- Because I believe complaint pleads facts sufficient to establish my claims, it would not be futile to provide me the opportunity to cure any defects the court may find in the complaint

- I have not amended complaint prior

Our response was filed on April 25, 2014 and defense's reply was filed on May 5, 2014.

And just like 'it is not over until the fat lady sings,' in law, it is not decided until the Judge rules. The Judge can take as long as s/he wants or needs to rule on the motion and there is no rushing the Judge. There was nothing to do now but to wait.

Judge's Order and Opinion on Motion to Dismiss

In the Motion to Dismiss stage, the court's job is to evaluate the adequacy of the complaint and not the evidence. The order and opinion states the totality of the circumstances alleged in my complaint and all the reasonable inferences that flow from them. It suggests the discrimination I allegedly experienced at the company was sufficiently severe or pervasive to alter the conditions of my employment for the worse.

Allegations of material fact in the complaint are taken as true and construed in the light most favorable to the nonmoving party. To be assumed true, the allegations "may not simply recite the elements of a cause of action, but must contain sufficient allegations of underlying facts to give fair notice and to enable the opposing party to defend itself effectively"

To avoid dismissal, a plaintiff must plead facts sufficient to "state a claim to relief that is plausible on its face. A claim has facial plausibility when the plaintiff pleads factual content that allows the court to draw the reasonable inference that the defendant is liable for the misconduct alleged."

In September of 2014, I received the news that defendant's Motion to Dismiss was in large part denied. This is not a very unusual verdict since it is typical that the plaintiff gets this win.

Some of the rulings of interest include:

- My claim that my company twice failed to promote me 6 years prior because of my religion was time-barred. The order and opinion referenced a case declaring "discrete discriminatory acts (to include failure to promote) are actionable only if they are not time barred-even where they are part of a series of discriminatory acts that includes acts that are not time barred.

- In response to defense saying the majority of my claims involve Christmas-related activities, not religion, the court said this argument lacked merit. Title VII defines the term "religion" to include "all aspects of religious observance and practice, as well as belief." The court agreed with me that a statement about "the birth of Christ," Crosses on the holiday party invitations and a song with lyrics, "Christ our Lord," all contain an aspect of religious observance, practice or belief.

- The order and opinion confirmed our statement, "The court must give liberal construction to the EEOC charge as it is often drafted by lay individuals not expert in drafting formal pleadings, and therefore not held to the same strict pleading requirements of a complaint," by stating "courts liberally construe charges that were not prepared by lawyers."

- The court responded to the company's argument that I did not exhaust my administrative remedies with respect to my hostile work environment because nothing of the sort is indicated on my charge. The court determined that not only is there no box to check on the EEOC intake form to declare Hostile Work Environment, but I sufficiently put the company on notice of this environment when I had numerous discussions with the CEO about the office 'culture.' The ruling continues to say that because I check marked the box next to continuing action and charged the company with having a culture that discriminated against me on the basis of religion, I had exhausted my administrative remedies.

- The court also disagreed with defense that I failed to prove I was subject to an adverse employment action because I had not been demoted or suffered a decrease in pay. The court stated the argument lacked merit since my complaint alleges that the company failed to promote me because of my religion which is an adverse employment action. It is further written in order and opinion that the level of harassment need not be "unendurable" or "intolerable," it need only be of such quality or quantity that a reasonable employee would find the conditions of her employment altered for the worse."

Disparate treatment and hostile work environment-defined

In short my claim alleged two causes of action against the company pursuant to Title VII of the Civil Rights Act of 1964: religious discrimination through disparate treatment and a hostile work environment and retaliation through disparate treatment.

Disparate treatment is defined as an employer treats some people less favorably than others because of their race, color, religion, sex or national origin.

Hostile work environment is not that simple.

My manager, who used the term 'hostile working environment' flippantly and inaccurately, was probably one of many people in all organizations who do so. She would use the term any time any member of the department would say or do something that appeared less than peaceful, calm, or agreeable. I learned from my lawsuit the term has a specific legal definition.

The Defendant's Motion to Dismiss, the Plaintiff's response, and the court's opinion and order all defined hostile work environment in more detail.

A hostile work environment claim may be actionable where an employee proves

- S/he was subjected to verbal or physical conduct of a harassing nature because of a protected characteristic

- This conduct was unwelcome

- The conduct was sufficiently severe or pervasive to alter the conditions of the victim's employment and created a work environment that a reasonable person would consider hostile or abusive."

It is the last of these three that framed my case.

Determining whether a hostile work environment claim is actionable, courts employ a totality of the circumstances test. In determining whether conduct was sufficiently severe or pervasive, courts must look at "all the circumstances" including

- Frequency of the discriminatory conduct

- Its severity

- Whether it is physically threatening or humiliating, or a mere offensive utterance

- Whether it unreasonably interfered with the performance of the employee's work.

A workplace is considered hostile when it is permeated with discriminatory intimidation, ridicule and insult that is sufficiently severe or pervasive to alter the conditions of the victim's employment. Offhand comments and isolated incidents are not enough. The sporadic use of abusive language and occasional teasing will not suffice to support a hostile work environment claim.

In order to prevail, the plaintiff must demonstrate a working environment that is both subjectively and objectively perceived to be abusive. Plaintiff must "show she perceived her work environment to be hostile and that a reasonable person in her position would perceive it to be so."

Once I learned the true definition of the term, I suggested to the Director of my department that he inform others in the company that the term should only be used in its legal sense.

More on Hostile work environment per the order and opinion on Motion to Dismiss:

Hostile environment claims are treated slightly differently than discrete disparate treatment claims. Because by their nature, hostile environment claims are usually based on 'the cumulative effect of individual acts' and not on any one event that occurred on a particular day. Courts use a 2 step analysis to determine if acts are part of a timely hostile environment claim.

They question if the acts are part of the same actionable hostile work environment practice and if so, does any act fall within the statutory time period?

"Courts consider whether the acts were sufficiently severe or pervasive and whether the various events amounted to the same type of employment actions, occurred relatively frequently, or were perpetrated by the same managers. The court's task is to determine if the events in the complaint that make up plaintiff's hostile environment claim are sufficiently linked to any of the prior events plaintiff alleges such that they form the same actionable hostile work environment practice."

Because the plaintiff does not need to support allegations with evidence as long as complaint alleges sufficient facts to satisfy each element of a hostile work environment claim, the court ruled in my favor claiming the alleged comments made by CM (the CEO) and HB (the manager) in 2012 are consistent with their earlier comments that form my hostile work environment claim.

All the comments arguably demonstrate the company's criticism or disapproval of (me) because of (my) religion. Their derogatory comments are part of the same allegedly hostile work environment practice so this issue is considered timely.

The court's denial of the Motion to Dismiss, while encouraging, turned out later to be nothing more than a pseudo triumph.

Now that defense was denied a Motion to Dismiss, they had to 'answer' the complaint within 21 days. It is a procedural formality and typically the defense denies any and all allegations as stated in the complaint. Once we received the answer document, the lawyers on both sides created a discovery schedule with end dates for many items including last day for witness list and completion of all depositions. After the court approved the schedule, Discovery began.

CHAPTER 4

Let the Litigants Begin Their Discovery

THE DISCOVERY PHASE is a pre-trial procedure in which each party can obtain evidence. Discovery methods include initial disclosures, interrogatories, request for admissions (RFA), request for production of documents (RFP), and depositions.

Discovery requests from Defense

- Interrogatories

The document states that the interrogatories are to be answered separately, fully, in writing and under oath. Thirty days are allowed to respond and send back to defense attorneys. There were 15 interrogatories mostly asking for detailed information on each of my claims. I wrote up my answers and gave them to my attorney who then formatted appropriately and sent them to the defense attorney

- Requests for Admissions

This is a list of items that I either mark *Admit* or *Deny*.

I admitted to everything except for the very last item: Admit that you never informed anyone at (company) that HB allegedly told you that you were "dead" because you didn't "reveal Jesus" to yourself.

Personal note: I always wondered if placing this last item was strategic-perhaps because my mark was continuing on admit, I would continue this as a habit-human nature!

- Requests for Production of Documents

This is much like the Interrogatories (of course from a lay person's view) except whereas the Interrogatories ask for written answers, the Production of Documents, as its name suggests, asks for the actual documents that confirm what was written in Interrogatories as well as documents we intend to use during discovery or trial phase.

Discoveries requested of Defense

We had first and second set of interrogatories with a total of 14 interrogatories sent to defendant. Each of their responses began with a boiler plate statement such as:

- Defendant objects on the grounds that the interrogatory contains multiple discrete subparts

- Defendant further objects on the grounds that the interrogatory is overly broad and unduly burdensome.

- Defendant objects on the grounds that the interrogatory is vague, ambiguous and calls for speculation

- Defendant objects on the grounds that the interrogatory seeks irrelevant information not reasonably calculated to lead to the discovery of admissible evidence

- Subject to and without waiving these objections, defendant responds as follows… (They proceeded to give a more precise and straight forward answer to the request).

We also had first and second set of requests for production of documents and tangible things to defendant with a total of 15 requests. Many were sufficiently answered-some not. Included in Defendant's documentation was the 'initial disclosure statement' that "individuals likely to have discoverable information that the disclosing party may use to support its claims or defenses."

Incidentally, we also had to give our witness list at this time.

Most of the documents submitted by both the Defense and Plaintiff overlapped. We exchanged such documents as surveys from class attendees giving feedback on classes I taught, my file from EEOC, my performance reviews, emails including those about the anonymous letter and compliments I received, the company handbook, and other benign items. In fact, the most negative item was the anonymous letter.

Depositions

Here are some things you want to know about depositions:

The deposition needs to be taken very seriously. It is much like a trial in that the deposed swears under oath to tell the truth and a court reporter records the questions and answers. Only one person on the opposing side can ask questions. There is no judge though, so all questions must be answered even if the attorney for the deposed objects. If the case goes to trial, the Judge will then decide if the question/answer is admissible. The deposition can be read in court. You can only be deposed once per case. I am offering information on depositions and tips for the deposed. While these work for depositions, many of the items below also work well in everyday communication and interaction.

- As the attorney representing the opposing party, they are inclined to use the deposition to:

  » Find out all you know and your perspective on the situation

  » Perhaps catch you in contradictory statements, lies, omissions so your credibility will be in question if you go to trial

  » Get ammunition to prepare for testimony should it go to trial

  » Retrieve information damaging to you and helpful to their client

- You are sworn under penalty of perjury; the deposition has the force and effect as if you were testifying in a court of law.

- If you testify at a later point and it contradicts something you have said in the deposition, the transcript may be used to impeach your further testimony.

- Since it is being recorded, accuracy is important so neither the examiner nor the deposed should speak 'over' the other. Let the question as well as the answer be complete and totally audible. Speak loudly and clearly.

- The attorney (examiner) may have many documents s/he uses for questioning. Be sure you read each of these and check they are accurate as you know it.

- You are only obligated to give facts that are within your personal knowledge. You are not required to give speculations, impressions or beliefs.

- Deposed can receive a copy of the transcript and can make changes which gives attorneys the opportunity to use those changes in front of a judge/jury.

- It is totally acceptable during the deposition to adjust something you had already said.

- Sometimes opposing counsel will 'win' a few.

When being questioned if an email I sent out about an article my daughter had published in a local newspaper violated company policy referring to not using company equipment for personal emails, I stated I did not violate the policy to which he responded, "but you agree this is not work related, right?" Ok, I had to give him this one!

- You can ask for a break any time during the process unless it is the space between the question and the answer. You may want to let them know you want a break as soon as you answer the question.

- You are always allowed to speak in private with your attorney.

- Remember, the end of the deposition is just as important as the beginning.

What you want to know about depositions-some tips on behavior protocol by the deposed:

- If asked a 'yes' or 'no' question, you can answer with just a 'yes' or 'no.' Say just what you need to say and stop talking when you are finished. If the opposing counsel needs more information, they will ask for it. If the answer is neither 'yes' nor 'no' say so.

- If you cannot recall something, state "I do not recall at this time." The latter 3 words are important in case you do go to trial and then recall.

- Don't worry how many times you can't recall something. Our experiences aren't held in a vacuum-they are embedded in an array of actions, conversations and events. We don't have a life highlight marker to draw attention to these items nor do we have the proverbial crystal ball letting us know this will be important information down the road.

- Don't guess. If you don't know the answer, just say so. Estimates are fine if you don't have exacts. I knew things happened within the first 6 months of 2011 although did not have exact dates/times.

I often answered questions such as "do you know whether or not they intentionally included a picture that had a Cross on it?" with "I wouldn't know that."

- Answer only the question asked. Resist the impulse to volunteer additional information. The answer should not exceed the question. Be cooperative while not 'spilling too many beans.'

- Answer only specific questions. If the question is too general, ask attorney to be more specific.

I was asked, "Do you remember anything else that was discussed with you and Mr. C during that conversation?" I answered, "About this topic?" Attorney responded affirmatively to which I replied, "No, there was nothing more."

- Do not answer unless you are 100% sure of what the questioner is asking. If you are not clear about the question, ask for it to be repeated, rephrased, or clarified. If you don't do any of those, the opposing attorney can justly assume you understand the question and are "answering to the best of your abilities."

- Give the facts as you know them and abstain from justifying your knowledge of them. You don't need to explain the process by which you reached the answer.

- Be honest and tell the truth (as you know it). You are under oath - perjury is a felony.

- Give a bit of space between the question and your answer. Think it through to answer most effectively. Leaving a bit of air space also allows your attorney the chance to object.

- Be sure you are clear if you are paraphrasing or quoting.

When I wasn't sure of the exact statement made by another, I circumvented direct quoting using statements such as, "they said something to the effect of…" or "they either said___or___"

- Make accurate any inaccuracies the opposing attorney may say in question or in summation. Be sure your story is neither twisted nor words are put into your mouth. It is ok to say, "I didn't say that."

When opposing counsel was questioning about the Cross on the holiday party invitation, he showed an exhibit of an email sent out about decorating our cubicles. One graphic used was a Menorah. He asked if this was ok on an invitation. I made it accurate by saying this was not an invitation but an email about how we might decorate. There is a difference.

The defense attorney made the comment, "well, you weren't intending to go to HR to complain about it, were you." He was referencing my dissatisfaction with the holiday party of 2011. While I never said I wasn't intending to go to HR, he went ahead and made this assumption anyway.

- If there is silence after answering a question, don't be compelled to fill dead air. Someone will eventually break the silence and it needn't be you.

- Acknowledge and answer the question directly while using it as an opportunity to use it as a bridge to state what you want the other side to know. It very well may be a statement you made previously. This is a good time to draw more attention to it.

- Have boundaries on what you will say. Opposing counsel may keep asking the question over and over again (usually in a different way and at a different point in the deposition). If you have nothing to add, just keep repeating your same answer.

- Your demeanor is very important. Be in total control of your tone, behavior, and attitude.

- Get good night's sleep.

I rarely get headaches yet after 5 ½ hours of being questioned, I needed a few Advil.

- Be prepared for many 'why' questions.

Being asked 'why' so many times, I appreciated the value of my encouraging clients to ask more 'what' questions than 'why.' Why is very invasive and accusatory. Because of such, they work well for the questioning attorney. I find in my life I don't always know <u>why</u>.

If you have ever been involved in any part of a lawsuit-or just watch T.V. for that matter, you know one states, "I swear to tell the truth..." And that is the biggest lie ever told.

Background: I made a complaint about my manager letting me know I was dead because I didn't reveal Jesus to me (or some iteration of this). All the antics involved in this area give me reason to call this a company version of The Comedy of Errors (thank you Mr. Shakespeare) or at the very least, material for a sitcom episode.

The way it was- otherwise known as the truth:

Sometime in the first 6 months of 2011 at a department meeting my manager looked at me and said something to the effect that I was dead because I didn't allow Jesus to reveal himself to me. Her arm was on the table in close proximity to me so I put my hand over her arm and informed her that it was merely a belief of hers, I do not believe that, I have never revealed Jesus to me and never will and I am fine with that. I proceeded to tell her she must abstain from ever saying that to me again. I walked out of the meeting with my co-worker, SR, and we made mention of this as we approached our cubicles. I proceeded to tell the HR Director. She did seem upset about it and she said she would talk to the CEO. I left there and went to speak with my co-worker, MS, who in her deposition reminded me that I told her the HR Director did not take notes. With my memory jogged, I did then clearly remember wondering in my meeting with the HR Director why she wasn't taking notes. I went back to the HR Director a couple of weeks after I first told her about the statement and asked her if she spoke with the CEO and she responded she had met with him only to let him know there may be religious issues going on. She clearly stated she did not tell him who said what.

So here is where the Comedy of Errors begins. In their interrogatories (interrogatories need to be truthful also), defense wrote that in '09 or '10 I did report that HB allegedly made a comment relating to religion that offended a non-Christian co-worker. My deposition started with questioning about the egregious comment HB said to me in 2011 about being 'dead' and then the question was juxtaposed with the incident that happened with my co-worker prior to this incident. I cleared it up with my answer that the episode he was referencing happened in '08 when my manager discussed her religious belief system with MS (my co-worker) and me. I continued to state that I tuned her out although my co-worker was upset with the monologue. I never remembered telling the HR Director. If I did, I am sure it was in passing.

The interrogatory continued to state that the HR Director spoke with the manager, HB, and made sure no such alleged comments were made in the future.

In her deposition, the manager in question testified she had a discussion with the HR Director (she believed) about not discussing religion in the workplace and the HR Director did not specifically tell her not to talk about religion in the workplace. Perhaps the HR Director did speak with the manager although I was never informed.

Ok-the plot is beginning to thicken. Furthermore, defense wrote in the interrogatory, "the matter was resolved, and plaintiff never made any future complaints about HB ever making any other alleged of-fensive comments concerning religion." Maybe the issue of '08 was resolved but the rest of this statement is an extreme falsehood. I did complain again-remember how in 2011 she told me I was dead...? The year 2011 is after 2009 or '10.

It gets even better. Enter the then COO who learns about the state-ment made to me when I told him such at a meeting he and I were having. He asked if it was resolved and I told him not as far as I was concerned because no one got back to me. The interrogatory falsely states I did not request nor comment that any further action was needed at that meeting. CM testified in his deposition that shortly after that meeting he met with the then CEO and asked him if he was aware of the incident and if he felt it was resolved. Per the testi-mony, RB, the then CEO, answered affirmatively. The COO also tes-tified he had no recollection of the verbiage either I or the then CEO used to state it was resolved. Did I mention that in her deposition, the HR Director testified she first heard of the 'dead' comment when I filed the lawsuit? So in 2012 the then CEO knew about the incident and decided it was resolved even though (per the HR Director), she did not know about it until 2014 and she would be the only person who would have knowledge of it to tell the CEO. Additionally, when the manager was asked if she made the comment, she answered simply, "no."

If you were following me, here is the short version. There are two distinct situations taking place 3 years apart yet intermingled by the company. The manager who said the 'dead' statement denies ever saying it, the HR Director claims she first heard about it when the lawsuit was filed, the CEO (then COO) says I stated the issue was resolved (never said that) and that the then CEO said it was resolved even though the manager said it never happened and the HR Director said she did not know anything about it. Did I also mention I told the then COO I had witnesses? One of those witnesses did testify the manager indeed said that to me at a meeting. She also testified that I did go to speak with the HR Director immediately after the incident.

Oh-there is more. In Summary Judgment it was accurately stated I reported this incident to the HR Director. Here comes the lie: defense's Summary Judgment states that the HR Director promptly investigated the matter and met with both HB and the then CEO. The lie continues saying HB (the manager) was then informed that religious based comments …were unacceptable. Yet, the HR Director testified she first learned about this in the lawsuit so per her testimony, she could not have promptly investigated it. HB testified she never said it and was not specifically told not to mention it again.

> **"Oh what a tangled web we weave, when first we practice to deceive"**
>
> -Sir Walter Scott

Will the real story please stand up? The real story is mine. When a Christian person who is your manager says to you, a Jewish person, you are dead because you didn't reveal Jesus to you, there are two absolutes here:

1. I could never make up that story (it was easier for the manager to lie and say "no" than for me to fabricate this incident in part or whole)

2. I could never forget that incident.

Finale: The only reason the manager never said that religious belief statement to me again was not at all that the company did their job; it was because I definitively told the manager to never say that to me again. The company did nothing; I took care of it.

When you are dealing with something as serious as a manager telling an employee that she is dead because she did not reveal Jesus to her, you better be able to present documentation that it was remedied. CM could not iterate the exact, or close to exact, statements either I or the then CEO, RB said indicating the issue was resolved. He had no clue what specifically was done to satisfy my issues. With an issue this serious, no one contacted the CEO, RB, at time of lawsuit to get clarity on it (to my knowledge).

You are probably wondering how so many lies could be told when under oath. Well, there was one statement said under oath that was true. When the CEO was asked to give his overall opinion of me as an employee of this company, he stated I was "intelligent and a talented trainer." True.

CHAPTER 5

Ending the case

Summary Judgment

A MOTION FOR Summary Judgment can be submitted by either party or both although usually done by defense. In my case, only defense filed the motion. Once they filed, we filed a response and then they filed their reply to the response.

Never think that upstanding ethics and morals get in the way of defense telling falsehoods and manipulating data from testimonies. Take a look at how defense had no problem changing what was testified and changing facts to lies.

- Defense stated that when I received the holiday party invitation of 2011 I "wasn't even sure that it had a Cross on it and had to check with a co-worker."

What my testimony in my deposition states is that I asked DP (my coworker) "it is a Cross, right? There is a Cross on this invitation, right?" I had someone acknowledging what I was seeing. I never said I was not sure that it had a Cross on it.

- In regards to the anonymous letter, defense wrote in the

Summary Judgment, "Rich was extremely defensive and re-fused to accept the advice offered by (the manager) because the letter was anonymous and not credible." Again, the inci-dent got totally twisted. I did tell the manager the letter had no credibility. While there was nothing she advised that I did not know already, there was no indication or proof I did not accept her advice or that I was defensive.

- Summary Judgment states "the letter was from a student from one of her classes…" I had already testified that there was no proof of this and yet defense was presumptuous enough to state this as incontrovertible fact.

- Regarding the 'religious' holiday party they footnoted, "no-tably Rich could have assisted in creating and/or suggesting holiday party decorations but failed to do so."

Yet I clearly stated in my deposition that the holiday party was kept a secret from all of us by the two managers who were organizing the party. Defense continued to ask, "what about the decorations, was that a surprise?" I responded, "Everything was a surprise." Therefore, I have no idea why he claims in Summary Judgment I could have as-sisted. The two managers never solicited participation in planning.

- They wrote "rich fails to discuss the fact that an investiga-tion was promptly conducted by HR Director (regarding the statement about my being dead). I did not fail to mention it because I was never told or informed of an investigation. I cannot tell that which I do not know.

- They continued to defy all testimonies and claim the compa-ny took 'remedial measures' concerning the 'dead' statement that were clearly effective since I never complained again of HB making any alleged improper comments. They continued to say, "Effective action was taken immediately to resolve her complaint"

I clearly testified there were no remedial measures taken and the only reason her comments stopped was because I told her to stop saying things like that to me. They did nothing to resolve my complaint. Although she lied under oath, the HR Director testified she did not know about the comment until the lawsuit was filed. How could effective action been taken if she did not know?

- In a footnote on their Summary Judgment referring to my stating the email I sent about Chanukah was not personal, they wrote, "rather than acknowledge the email was not in violation of the policy and move on, Rich instead vigorously argued the email was not in violation of the policy…" I did not vigorously argue – in fact I did not argue at all. When defense asked if my testimony was that I did not violate the policy, I responded, "my testimony is that I did not violate the policy." That is hardly an argument and even as a statement, I find the adverb vigorously to be vigorously overstated (see what I did there?).

- Regarding my meeting with the HR Director about the manager's behavior at our department meeting, the Motion also states, "(HR Director) agreed she would talk to (HB) about making it optional for any (trainer) to have to share their work goals with other team members.

I never said anything about goals; ironically in her notes, the HR Director quotes me saying the name of my co-worker for whom the goal topic was an issue.

- Summary Judgment states that I was never offered a Poinsettia again. That is true although it was not because of anything about me. Actually, the company never gave them again due to direction from the Board of Directors (as was told to the employees). Summary Judgment states that the first manager who wanted to give me the Poinsettia did give it to another employee. This is inaccurate; I gave it to MS (co-worker) and I told the HR person in my email that I would be doing that.

- And then their Summary Judgment offered a Surprise!

Background information: Because I was asked so often in deposition 'why' I did not report incidences to the HR Director, I went to her 4 months after I was deposed to report a terrible occurrence of my manager behaving 'off the wall' at our department meeting. I stated to the HR Director what happened and she said she would talk to others in the meeting to confirm. I know she spoke with one of the three others who verified-if not more, what I claimed happened in that meeting. She also spoke with the manager. At my initial meeting with the HR Director about this crisis, she asked me to write up our meeting which I did-only to get stabbed in the back, as the saying goes.

The surprise: It not only went into my personnel file – which I understand- but the company turned it all around and included it, albeit at the 11th hour, in my case. Nothing in this incident had anything to do with my case or discrimination. It did not address or refute anything in my charge, complaint, or deposition. Its only function was to defame my character. To use it against me well after my deposition and with no warning that it be used in Summary Judgment is not only callous but hypocritical. After all, they complained how I didn't let them know until filing with EEOC about my claim of discrimination. I don't blame the attorney-he was just doing his job; the company is thoroughly responsible for this heinous 'pull a rabbit out of the hat' trickery.

I don't know which is sadder-that defense was granted Summary

Judgment in light of their flagrant manipulation of data or that the company was complicit and allowed fallacious information to be stated, key facts to be unstated, and outlandish descriptions of me to be public via the federal court system.

The final ruling

My reaction to the ruling on Summary Judgment was a combination of relief and disappointment. I was relieved that it was over and I had the answer, albeit, not the one for which I was hoping. I was disappointed that the Judge granted Summary Judgment to defense in its entirety. Had he denied defense even one item, the case would have continued and hopefully defense would have decided a dialogue would have been a good option. If not, we would have gone to trial where I would have been given a chance to tell my story directly to the judge and jury.

Advice I often give people is to limit online communication and talk in person. The indirect methods of text messaging and email lend themselves to back and forth chat that gets caught in the realm of confusion, misunderstanding and muddle. This is exactly how I saw the documents that both attorneys wrote up. Just like I tell clients to talk face to face, I felt I deserved to do so and get my day in court.

Yes, relief and disappointment but certainly not surprise. I was told by several attorneys from several states as well as friends and family that I would have a difficult time winning my case in a red state. Notoriously it is the employer and not the employee who wins in such. When I read the Judge's ruling on the Motion to Dismiss, I had to disagree with those who told me I would lose in Arizona. Then I read the order and opinion on Summary Judgment. Indeed, I was an employee in a red state. I was cut no slack whatsoever. Defense was granted Summary Judgment in its entirety.

You are probably saying, "He is a Judge and goes by what the law says." Of course knowing the law very well could be a double edged sword. It is then easy to know where all the arguments are that substantiate your pre-conceived theory. Ok, now you are probably saying, "He is a Judge and he is unbiased. After all, justice is blind." This is hopefully true. However, as a member of the human species s/he, like all others, works from a place of personal values, experiences, and beliefs that are often set in the subconscious. We avoid having those areas challenged by opposing position. They guide us. The human being in us innately seeks out information that supports the opinions we hold. And no matter what our profession is or job obligations entail, we cannot ignore their grip on us.

It goes back to my theory about coffee. So to be unbiased, here are my findings on why coffee is bad for you…wait, I am digressing-back to topic at hand.

If you are thinking, "Well, we can't pick our judges," you are not entirely correct. Federal Judges across the country, not just Supreme Court Justices, are appointed by the President of the United States. My Judge was appointed by George H.W. Bush. I am not suggesting there is any cause and effect-just stating facts. If you want to choose your judge-VOTE.

The sad truth about Title VII

Employees are not safe against discrimination under Title VII and protections are far reaching.

Employers can and do discriminate. Workplaces of today are the South Shore Country Clubs of the 50's and 60's. They have just been modernized by voiding the blatant visibly displayed signs saying, "NO JEWS <u>PROMOTED</u>"

Defense stated that my allegations did not involve the extreme type of conduct necessary to establish a hostile work environment because they do not come anywhere near the level of the extreme conduct necessary to alter the terms and conditions of my employment. They cited several cases of people being subjected to disdainfully bigoted and prejudicial statements and conduct far more severe than what I claimed. In each of the cases cited, the ruling favored the employer saying the incidents were not severe or pervasive enough as a matter of law to establish a hostile work environment.

Defense used these cases to show the events I described as discriminatory were nowhere near the severity or pervasiveness as the other cases that failed the test of legal discrimination. Defense justifiably said that I did not explain why my claim should proceed when cases involving far more serious allegations were dismissed because the conduct did not give rise to a viable hostile work environment and I did not identify a single case where the alleged conduct was even remotely similar to my allegations and the case was permitted to proceed to trial.

I agree with defense on this one-my events did not reach the level of disgust as the others. I can't imagine what then would be severe or pervasive enough.

I find it burdensome and sad that someone has to endure such painful abuse and excessive humiliation before the court will determine actions discriminatory. The bar is set quite high and events need to rise to an extreme level of threat and humiliation. I am far from convinced that had someone placed a swastika in my office and saluted, "Heil Hitler" every day that I could then persuade the court I was discriminated against by not being promoted.

Defense also claimed that since I was not subjected to an abusive environment on a daily basis for the 12 years of my employment with this company, I cannot claim hostile work environment. Let me see if I have this straight. To claim hostile work environment, one must be abused by the company every day for many years. I don't see this as a means to declare discrimination. This is a cause for the company to be out of business!

General civility code

As I was informed, there is a rhyme and reason that the Supreme Court set stringent standards for a case to be legally established as a hostile work environment. They want to ensure federal law does not become a 'general civility code' in the workplace. In other words, the Supreme Court is making sure issues that are not severely damaging are resolved at the organizational level.

And it is at the organizational level that my situation should have been addressed and concluded. Organizations have the onerous responsibility to be proactive and have systems, strategies, and structures in place to prevent any issues to be viewed as prejudicial, bias, or inhumane as well as ways of dealing with these issues if they occur.

If bias, prejudice and anti-Semitism are all business related issues and not legalities, then it is the responsibility of the company to address it with the person. Never, never, never should a company push forward with a situation so that it becomes a federal court case when it can be avoided easily and productively at the organizational level.

PART 2
BIGOTRY AND RELIGION

CHAPTER 6

Christmas is Not About Being Jewish

WHILE CHRISTMAS IS a one day holiday celebrated religiously by Christians, the season takes on a whole different celebration. Separating the one day holiday from the season shapes the difference between acceptable and unacceptable in the workplace. From around Thanksgiving to the beginning of the following year, most people participate in activities of joyfulness, fun, benevolence, and merriment. To achieve any or all of these, people will engage in festivities such as parties, holiday decorating, and volunteering for charitable organizations. These are all non-religious. Companies decorate for the holiday season with Christmas trees, wreaths and nutcrackers to name a few. It is a heartwarming scene.

I have always enjoyed the holiday season.

For several years my daughters and I volunteered at a food bank where we packaged food items during the Christmas season. Afterward we went to a holiday party at the person's house who designed the whole day. We so enjoyed our taking part in this worthwhile endeavor.

As a teen, my friends (all Jewish) and I would drive through a neighborhood richly decorated for Christmas so we could marvel at the ingenuity that created the beauty adorning the front yards. Many oohs and aahs along with favorable adjectives were uttered in our car.

For 22 of the past 23 years I have always attended the Christmas party of one of my Catholic friends. Her house and yard are completely decorated for the holiday. I always marvel at how stunning the holiday décor is and I get mesmerized by her exquisitely decorated floor to ceiling tree.

I always heard that Midnight Mass was a breathtaking service. I mentioned this to the novice whom I was observing as a teacher as part of my college studies. She invited me to attend Midnight Mass that year with her and the other Nuns. I did and was in awe. Interesting, the first song they sang was in Hebrew.

The Christmas season is for all of us even in the workplace. It is only when the season mingles too deeply with the religious component that it becomes inappropriate.

When I worked for an international fortune 100 company in the late 80's, our location was positioned with a tall and fashionably adorned Christmas tree in the middle of the lobby. It was a stunning attraction- until someone placed a rather big nativity scene under it. I asked the Senior Manager to remove it because it was quite religious. No questions asked. The nativity scene was immediately removed.

Defense in my case said my lawsuit rested on events during the Christmas season only. This does not minimize its effect. No season offers leniency or amnesty of anti-Semitism.

I never questioned the activities the company implemented to bring out the joy of the holiday season. Having holiday pot luck lunches, decorating cookies, adorning our cubicles, contributing to a charitable cause, having a secret Santa week, as well as holiday parties were never anathema to me. It was not until the company crossed the line between the season of Christmas and the religious holiday of Christmas that I found the season less joyful.

The holiday party of 2011 posed a Christian Cross on the invitation. I immediately told the HR Director about this-not to complain but I thought it would be best that she knew so it would not cause problems for the company from anyone. It was photo shopped out although the hard copy of the invitation would always display the Cross.

The party itself had strong undertones of religion including having carolers who sang religious songs that had phrases such as "Christ our Lord." I was extremely uncomfortable while the carolers were going around to tables and singing such verses while in very close proximity to me. My discomfort was noticeable and evident. One person at my table asked if I was ok and a co-worker at the table next to mine called out to me, "Maybe they will sing one of your songs" (something like that). She also added, "sorry, Marcy" when she requested a religious Christmas song. As I walked to the back of the room at some point, I stopped at a table where a co-worker friend of mine was sitting next to the COO, CM. I made a comment to him about how Christian the party was and CM looked me directly in the eye. It was a look of either recognition or inquiry. In either case, I was sure he learned quickly of my concern. My manager was informed from her manager of my dissatisfaction so she asked me about it. I relayed to her my feelings and she responded only with "interesting."

Word got around that I did not view this party favorably and still no one in senior management or in Human Resources contacted me to discuss further.

CHAPTER 7

What is Offensive is What is Being Judged

> **"You never really understand a person until you consider things from his point of view...until you climb in his skin and walk around in it."**
>
> - Harper Lee in *To Kill a Mockingbird*

The difference between being offended and being judged

THE WORD *OFFEND* in some iteration in regards to religion was repeatedly used in my deposition-worthy of the keyword for a vodka shot. If you read my deposition, be prepared for a minimum of 50 shots!

I was asked if a Christian person would have been *'offended'* with the Menorah on the email sent out by the company about decorating for the holidays. I answered, "I wouldn't know." For the most part, I don't know what specifically would *offend* a Christian person although I am very sure the company would hear from its employees if in a non-denominational environment, Christians were asked to kiss the Mezuzah each time they entered a room where the artifact was placed on the doorposts, if each man had to wear a yarmulke all day, or that the kitchen was strictly kosher so only foods marked with a *k* or a *u* to indicate it is kosher would be allowed. Shellfish and pork would not be allowed and milk and meat could not be mixed.

A *Facebook* friend of mine who is African American posted that a white person appearing in 'black face' is offensive to an African American person. If I were asked the converse, would a black person appearing in white face offend me I would answer, "I think it is distasteful although I may not feel offended." Why? Because there is no abhorrent history for me regarding 'white face.' I have no anchor or reference point for it as a black person would have about the concept of 'black face.' Just because something that offends someone does not offend another, does not void the power the offense has. Additionally, no one should be judged on what offends them or told they shouldn't be offended.

It is not about being offended. Whether I was offended or not is insignificant. If I am offended, it is my problem. It goes way beyond offense. It is about being judged and examined for one's beliefs.

Poinsettia Plant

One of the issues I presented was about being offered Poinsettias. Twice the company was giving them out at Christmas time, twice I requested giving mine to my co-worker, and twice I was rudely interrogated and judged for not accepting the plant.

I was never sure why I had to go through this cross examination a second time since immediately after the first time I had a discussion about it with the HR person that included the story behind the Poinsettia that directly links it to Christmas.

I would have been happy to explain my decision to not accept the plant had they inquired in an attempt to learn. Giving Poinsettias was not the problem; interrogating and judging was.

Paper Plates

One of the projects I had was to lead a group of outside trainers who would help train our subscribers in exchange for their own business visibility and added value. To show our appreciation we had a luncheon for them during the Christmas holiday season. One particular year my manager had leftover Christmas holiday plates and asked if I wanted to use them. I wasn't comfortable using them since I considered the purpose of the luncheon was to thank these people for assisting us which had nothing to do with the holiday. I suggested we use neutral plates. She gave me a very disgusted look. A couple months later I told the then COO, CM, about this episode and without even seeing the plates, he stated, "I don't agree." While he has the prerogative to agree or disagree, he is not offered the privilege of making his view equate to my being wrong. It is not his place, or anyone else's to determine what makes someone uncomfortable with items unaligned with his/her religious beliefs. Perhaps if he added to his biased statement something like, "however, we will honor your request" he would have done the company a better service. The paper plates was not the problem; judging and discounting someone's religious views was.

(Note: That year we did use neutral plates although 2 years later for the same group for which I was still a lead, I was not asked what type of plates I would like to have and my manager went ahead and used Christmas holiday plates. I testified I thought it was intentional-I would still testify that)

Christmas Plates-No Crosses but Christmas decoration.

Chanukah Plates-No Stars of David but Chanukah decoration

Neutral Plates

The solution was simple-they needed to learn from Santa Claus and a sales clerk at a novelty store.

When my younger daughter was about 4 years old, I took her shopping at Woodfield Mall in Schaumburg, IL where we lived then. It was Christmas time and Santa was present. As my daughter and I were walking through the mall, Santa came toward us and upon reaching our location, he got down on one knee and asked my daughter, "What do you want for Christmas?" Being wise beyond her years, she quickly replied, "I don't celebrate Christmas." Santa wasted no time and immediately rerouted his question to, "what do you want for Chanukah?" There was no interrogation, discounting or judgment-just respect.

Later that same season I took my 8 year old daughter and her friend to the same mall where we stopped in a home decorating store that unknown to me was kindly giving out a Christmas tree ornament to each customer. I graciously accepted it as I gave it to my daughter's Christian friend. The salesperson observed this, made a correct interpretation of it, and offered me a non-denominational figurine. There was no interrogation, discounting, or judgment-just respect.

And that is how it needs to be done!

CHAPTER 8

When Honoring Others is the Only Answer

Determining what others should believe

THE ISSUES OF the Poinsettia and paper plates found themselves in my deposition and in Summary Judgment.

In their Summary Judgment, defense said I wanted to give the Poinsettia to one of my co-workers who apparently during the lawsuit was flagged as a non-practicing Christian. My interpretations of this was that why should I not accept the Poinsettia and a non-practicing Christian does. First, there is no correlation and second, the important part of her description is the noun: Christian and not the adjective: non-practicing. The point here is what she does is her decision and what I do is my decision. We should never be held to the standard of someone else in our beliefs. It is presumptuous for anyone to insinuate I was wrong as a Jew to not welcome the Poinsettia when a 'non-practicing' Christian would accept it.

With their obsession of the Christian Cross, defense would question if something I claimed to be Christian had a Cross. Defense asked me if the paper plates had a Cross on them. Was he thinking I should have had no concern about using the plates since they did not have a Cross? In fact he often asked during my deposition if certain items such as emails, gifts and more had a Cross on them. The absence of a Cross on anything would not have minimized my concern that I was having other's religious beliefs placed on me with other Christmas symbols.

Defense referenced an image of a Menorah in an email from the company talking about decorating for the holidays. They compared the Menorah to a Cross. A Menorah is not analogous to a Cross. They pointed out that the Menorah on this email was greater in size than the Cross on the holiday invitation.

Wait for it…size does not matter!

There are several times in documents and deposition that defense referred to my statement that the Menorah had deep religious meaning. To be accurate, defense did not refer to it, defense totally mocked me on this. If this is how I see the artifact, then my choice should be honored and not put up for ridicule. My manager was well known to relentlessly mention her "Lord and Savior." While her saying this continually may have been annoying at times, no one directly taunted her. I deserved the same respect.

The Hora, a dance, became an issue. One year I sent an email to staff that I would teach the Hora. Defense questioned me about this and also commented on it in Summary Judgment. My email stated it was a celebratory dance and did not equate it with Judaism at all. In my deposition I mentioned that it actually has its origin from other ethnic groups. The dance, having only three steps-jump, kick and grapevine-is far from anything religious and I am sure no one ever would be offended by it. In fact, my Zumba® instructors often choreograph using some combination of those steps. Yes, they are rather universal. Would I have been questioned the same if I were instructing the Salsa or Tango or even break-dancing?

Gifts

The gift giving and receiving part of the holiday season is always a joy-except when you receive a gift that you absolutely don't need, like or want. I know we may not always be cognizant of what others would enjoy receiving but sometimes it is simply a no-brainer. Getting something that is designed for Christmas to be used in the house is not something I dream of getting. Yet, the Director of Communications gave to each in her downline, a spoon rest that was Christmas decorated. No, it did not have a Cross (as defense would always ask) but it still was for Christmas. Of course this became an issue in my lawsuit and another means for defense to judge me. Would they have been happy receiving a Dreidel instead of a Poinsettia?

The gift I received was this spoon rest.

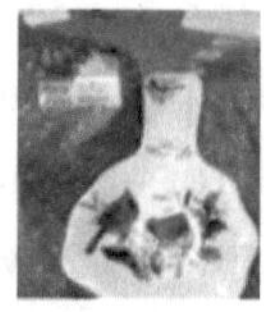

Would the employees have been happy receiving this Challah Cover?

CHALLAH COVER

I would never consider giving a Challah Cover to a Christian person. Sometimes we just have to stop and consider to whom we are giving what. It was kind of her to give me a gift but to give a gift that is something useless and meaningless to the receiver is not giving. We need to give a gift that is a fit for the other person. It is not giving if the gift is one that meets the giver's needs only. Remember the value of a gift is in the eye of the beholder. Always consider what is meaningful to the receiver.

One of my favorite stories relating to this is when I worked for the vendor of the company who was in the lawsuit. A co-worker had a Christmas catalogue that she was circulating around the office for all to see if they wanted to order anything. While she was combing through the 30 page book, she came across one page that had Chanukah gifts. In her excitement on finding this she said to me, "If I knew they had Chanukah things in here I would have ordered you something for Christmas!" Now there is someone who has much to learn.

Assimilating

Throughout history Jewish people have been forced or encouraged to assimilate.

During the Spanish Inquisition Jews were given three choices: convert to Christianity, get killed, or leave Spain.

Martin Luther, in the 16th century tried to convert Jews to Christianity through his reforms of Catholicism (and much more).

My grandparents, all of whom escaped the pogroms of Russia in the early 1900's, assimilated to be Americanized and leave behind the horror they had lived.

Many of the Jewish families in the community of my youth assimilated because they were learning about the atrocities inflicted on the European Jews during WWII and were doing what they could to be sure they would not be next.

Assimilation was a survival necessity.

So when the company had an invitation for the 2013 holiday party that displayed a Menorah with a nutcracker on each side of it showing an association of the two, I saw it not as an offense or insult but a strong mixed and incorrect message that was an affront and a slight to the Jewish people and religion.

It can be an uphill battle as we fight against assimilation so placing nutcrackers with the Menorah was extremely disrespectful. We never want to give the message that Chanukah is the Jewish Christmas. It is the ultimate irony and misunderstanding of Chanukah, which is the story of a fight against assimilation.

There was an episode of the television show Sex and the City that helps to explain this. One of the characters, Charlotte, a Christian woman was about to marry a Jewish man. She decided to convert to the Jewish religion and was going to classes in preparation of the conversion. After one of the classes she went up to the Rabbi, the class instructor, and asked if she could still have her Christmas tree. He said no and when seeing her consternation, continued with, "We have our own holidays."

The company was proud of themselves that they never again had a Cross on invitations or had live or recorded religious songs. In my deposition defense commented to me, "You allege they never took any steps to remedy the hostile environment. Wouldn't one thing been to not have Crosses anymore and not to have carolers? And they don't offer you a Poinsettia anymore" (for the record, the giving of Poinsettia's was totally abolished and had nothing to do with me). In the Summary Judgement again defense argued that the company "has taken steps in response to issues raised by Rich to try and ensure that no employee is offended by anything that occurs in the workplace."

They also curtailed activities and decorating for the holiday season. This last part discouraged me quite a bit since I had no intention to limit the seasonal enjoyment. I just wanted them to remove the religious aspect.

It is not about a Cross on an invitation or for that matter about a Poinsettia plant or about a bird on a spoon rest or holly on paper plates or a Menorah image larger than one of a Cross.

It is about being a Mensch, accessing the human being inside you and honoring each individual.

CHAPTER 9

It's Bigotry, No It's Prejudice, No It's...

WHETHER YOU CALL it prejudice, bias, or bigotry each can lead to anti-Semitism.

After the Judge's ruling, I have often been asked if I really believe I was discriminated against and a victim of anti-Semitism at the workplace. It is important to note that the Summary Judgment was granted to defense because, per the Judge, I did not have enough material fact to go before a jury. There is no statement that says defense didn't discriminate or that they are not anti-Semitic. There are no comments about right and wrong or win and lose. The Judge made his decision based on his knowledge of law and I rest my belief on my knowledge and experience of anti-Semitism. Perhaps in the world of federal law it was not discrimination. In my world it had many of the elements of anti-Semitism and discrimination.

Anti-Semitism, or any anti, is an attitude and can remain concealed until it transfers to a behavior.

I was in a poetry class in my freshman year of college at the University of Illinois in Urbana where I sat in a horizontal row with two of my friends, also Jewish. Each of us received a 'C' on our first paper. Well, we thought, typical, give the student a lower grade at first so they work harder for a higher grade. This seemed to us a practical strategy- until we continually received a letter grade of 'C' while others were recipients of the former strategy and received an 'a' or 'b.' One of the other two ladies decided to ask the teacher about this. She simply asked, "What is not good about my writing? What do I need to do to improve?" The instructor looked up at her and immediately re- sponded, "You Jews think you are so great. You have a chip on your shoulder and you better get it off." We hadn't considered her being anti-Semitic but now that she attached her attitude to a behavior we had no choice. Had my friend not spoken to her and heard her re- sponse, the teacher's anti-Semitism would not have been definitively expressed to us. However, whether she voiced it or not, she had a strong dislike for Jews-an attitude that was manifested in her behavior of giving us our grades. I suppose it is like: if a tree falls in the forest and no one is there, can it still be anti-Semitic (much poetic license used here!).

When I told my father about this episode, he wisely informed me, "Get used to it. You will have it your entire life."

Unless someone is wearing a swastika or a post it note saying, "I hate Jews" anti-Semitism does not always have a spotlight on it. Just the same, there is plenty of anti-Semitism in the world and reports show it is growing. There is certainly a possibility that the organization for which I worked did have a culture of anti-Semitism.

Recognizing Anti-Semitism is less what you learn and more what you experience and live. When I was around 10 years old we got the news from networks on television. One night I was watching the news in my parent's room and I had my first close up experience. The Jewish cemetery in a suburb of Chicago where my maternal great grandparents are buried had been vandalized by Nazis. Many tombstones had writings saying, "All Jews will be found here." I remember that incident well. It was scary for a 10-year-old to hear this. After all, I was already learning the horrors of the Holocaust from friends and Sunday school teachers. *The Diary of Anne Frank* was on the bookshelf in my house as well as on the shelves of others in my community. Ever since then, I always considered what would make a good hiding place.

In their Summary Judgment, defense proceeded to wrathfully label my behavior regarding meetings and email communication with the HR Director about my manager's deplorable behavior at a department meeting, as boorish and stated erroneously I was enraged with (HB's) suggestions and sent an angry tirade to (HR Director). I was not enraged by her suggestions but troubled by her odious behavior and the rude comments she made. Even still, I did not send an angry tirade. They sugar coated the behavior of the manager.

If it were the attorney saying this, perhaps I could attribute the theatrics to a technique he may have learned in law school.

However, it was not the attorney but the HR person who listed this item in her affidavit which she signed (on behalf of the company) and was notarized.

"**Half a truth is often a great lie**" -Benjamin Franklin

Summary Judgment did not at all reference the manager's unprofessional behavior at that meeting. Instead they glorified her by saying she "had a meeting with all (trainers) wherein HB outlined various best practices and guidelines for employees to utilize when performing their duties. The purpose was to create consistency among the team and provide (company) customers/subscribers with the best services possible." While the manager may have seen it this way, it certainly wasn't the reason I went to speak with the HR Director. What I spoke about was conveniently not addressed nor was the fact that the HR person told me to write up the meeting she and I had-which I did and which was then readjusted to meet the needs of defense.

The HR Director came to my office shortly after I sent the email to get clarity on a couple of items. For this meeting, defense wrote in Summary Judgement: "rather than acknowledging the outrageous and inappropriate comments made in the email, Rich only sought to justify them." Not true. Again, there was no mention that the manager did not acknowledge the outrageous and inappropriate comments she made in the meeting since it was she and not I to whom those terms correctly apply.

Only a Non Mensch company would be pleased with their performance of criticizing, betraying, and demeaning a current employee using a dearth of facts.

For me, this is the crux of anti-Semitism often depicted throughout history by means of caricaturing the Jew as the demon with a big nose and horns and the Christian as the angel with a halo and wings.

Never Again!

Just because the events in my case did not reach the level of abuse and humiliation dictated by law, it does not mean the company is acquitted of prejudice, intolerance, or bigotry. While none is technically illegal, none should ever be allowed to exist unchallenged. Organizations should not shy away from taking on their responsibility to the world in stopping injustices to others.

Whether or not anti-Semitism played an instrumental role in my not getting another job position, the company indisputably wronged me by treating me unfairly. While there were many opportunities for the CEO to change my job position, he never did. My charge and complaint were about not being promoted and not about no longer having Crosses on invitations or being given a Poinsettia. All I wanted was meaningful challenging work that fully utilized my skills. Unlike others, I was denied.

Part 3
Organizations and
The General Civility Code

CHAPTER 10

The Mensch Organization v the Non Mensch Organization

DID YOU EVER hear the expression, "you don't know someone until you live with that person?" Tweak that a bit and you have another truism, "you don't know a company until you are involved in a lawsuit with them." A lawsuit will give you a good picture of the fidelity and sincerity that is absent in the organization.

My lawsuit allowed me to see much of the leadership that was worthy of sharing so I could give better options to others.

Two types of leadership determine two types of organizations

- Mensch leadership makes a Mensch organization- one that is altruistically driven

Mensch leadership is about being wise, confident, and unafraid to do the right things for those they serve. These leaders have the best interest of the organization in mind over their personal interests. They have a clear vision for the organization that is embraced by the staff.

In a Mensch organization, leadership and authority is decentralized. Mutual responsibility is the norm.

Mensch leaders know it is an absolute necessity and duty to take responsibility for relationships in the organization.

Mensch leaders actively communicate across the organization, stay connected, and create engagement.

- Non Mensch leadership makes a Non Mensch organization- one that is ego centric

Non Mensch leadership is about being addicted to being right and having an 'I' focus. These leaders do not let their lack of leadership skills get in the way of making decisions that are not always in the best interest of the organization. They usually do not have a clear vision for the organization.

In a Non Mensch organization, leadership and authority is localized in 'one' person. Obedience is the normal behavior.

Non Mensch leaders allow toxins to permeate the organization

Non Mensch leaders allow the structure of the organization to be like silos. They don't connect with all parts of the organization.

The Solitary Non Mensch Leader

If you want something tainted and unprincipled, go alone.

If you want something honorable and unpolluted, go with others.

"It's lonely at the top" is a statement often used about the plight of senior leadership. It is only true though when a leader chooses the

Lone Ranger role in guiding the organization. During the discovery phase in my lawsuit we learned that the Board of Directors was not advised of the situation until it became a lawsuit. Then, per testimony, the members of the Board were given few details.

Unilateral decision making has the elements for disaster. There is a good reason why we have a 'check and balance' government. Major decisions need to be viewed from different angles from various people. A discrimination case is a serious matter. Determining to litigate should be a decision viewed by many.

The Board of Directors seemed to let two main factors slide. First, a Mensch board would have inquired why they were not told much earlier raising a red flag as to what else is being hidden from them. This though pales compared to their abdicating their responsibility to do an investigation of the issue of discrimination.

Think about all the sexual harassment cases that have been brought into the open. Constantly one hears about the investigations that company leadership embarks on to uncover the truth. How often do you hear of Police departments probing for information when there is a questionable incident among its employees? There is no place for a Lone Ranger in a discrimination matter. There is no place for a 'head in the sand' Board of Directors in a discrimination matter.

Mensch leaders know nothing much of value comes from just one.

Mensch companies have an insatiable quest to know the truth. It is a must for being committed to acting on the truth.

Mensch organizations function on trust

Mensch leaders know that organizations are no longer built on force and power. Leaders no longer serve when they use their power willfully and grimly in attempts to control others. The use of raw power may gain compliance but never commitment or respect.

Leadership is an outgrowth of character. Mensch leaders cultivate credibility by demonstrating competence, sincerity, and integrity. They care deeply, continually, and instinctively for people.

Did you know that when passengers on a flight find their tray tables to be dirty, they unconsciously or consciously have a picture in their heads that the captain might be slovenly in his flying the plane? While the correlation may not be accurate, the perception to the passenger is. As Tom Peters famously said, "Perception is all there is."

It is no different with companies. Once management, especially senior leadership, creates a workplace that is high on deceit and low on disclosure, many interpretations take hold and understandings get distorted. When your words don't match your actions or you fail to 'walk the talk,' you won't be trusted in the future. Trust lost is hard to recover.

The most grievous travesty of trust the company committed via the lawsuit was taking the information from the meeting I had with the HR Director concerning the ill behavior of my manager in our department meeting and using it against me in the lawsuit. They included unjustified descriptions of me as 'boorish' and said I made 'outrageous comments.' A Non Mensch organization has no problem sacrificing their integrity. It does not mind abusing the trust the employee has in the company. A Mensch organization would stand by their ethical principles of human decency and follow this policy even in the midst of a lawsuit.

Mixed messages and hypocrisy are credibility destructive. They are both signs of a lack of congruency and consistency. They only cause distrust and confusion. Mensch leaders have their thoughts, words and feelings in alignment with their actions. One of my favorite of the four agreements outlined in the book of that title by Don Miguel Ruiz is 'be impeccable with your word.' A few items Ruiz mentions that Mensch leaders follow include:

- Say only what you mean; realize that you can cause damage and harm with speaking carelessly, thoughtlessly or aggressively

- Impeccability of the word addresses the power of speaking with integrity and reminds us to think before we speak.

- Speak with integrity. Your word is your bond. Use the power of your word in the direction of truth.

Non Mensch leaders go 'willy nilly' with their thoughts, words and actions. Here are some examples of mixed messages and hypocrisies.

- The CEO told me I couldn't have the position to do staff development because "the managers were not ready for it." Yet, all managers went to Orlando for leadership training. Apparently they were ready to go to Orlando and get leadership training at great expense. I was not even asking for higher pay.

- In a footnote on their Summary Judgment referring to my stating the email I sent about Chanukah was not personal, they wrote, "rather than acknowledge the email was in violation of the policy and move on, Rich instead vigorously argued the email was not in violation of the policy..." Have you heard before, "people who live in glass houses shouldn't throw stones?" Rather than vigorously litigating this issue, the company should have moved on to work on remedying the problems. Besides, I did not argue it but when asked if I was testifying if I violated policy I said "my testimony is that I did not violate the policy." That was stating a position and was not an argument.

- In one of our meetings, the CEO, CM, addressed his concern about my changing work location. He was leery of my working with another employee already at that location because that employee and I had differing political and religious views. The hypocrisy? I asked to be moved from reporting to my manager who blatantly told me I was dead because I did not reveal Jesus to me, who constantly talked about her "Lord and Savior" and who wanted to teach the Bible (Christian one) in our department meetings. He said "no." Apparently the huge gap in different views here was not an issue. Side note: the employee, referred to here, and I got along extremely well. In fact, he turned out to be a huge supporter of mine during the majority of my discrimination charge and complaint.

- When CM was coming on board, he was going to be placed somewhere in support services. With HB being the director at that time of the whole department, it meant CM would report to her. Guess again. The then CEO, RB, went to HB and told her CM would not report to her so he was going to split the department and she got to choose if she wanted the training part or the help desk part. The hypocrisy here is a double whammy. RB initially told me the support services department did not have too many employees warranting a split into two departments. Yet he brought someone new into the company and split the department. The second hypocrisy here is the person who determined he did not want to report to HB is the same person, CM, who said in legal documents that I did not get to make the same decision about to whom I report.

- In written documents as well as in my deposition, defense argued my wanting to be placed in another position stating

I was never a manager in my career. It was hypocritical for them to go this route when several in management positions had never been managers earlier. We had one employee who began as the solo help desk person staying on the phones to address subscribers' questions. He eventually became a Director-not just a manager but a Director. Additionally, the person who was the Director of Support Services, KP, was initially hired not for his management or leadership skills but rather for his abilities and talents needed for the role of the position of Compliance Officer.

- Defense continually asked me why I did not go to HR yet the CEO, CM, testified he did not go to HR the entire time my charge was alive with EEOC.

Mensch organizations adhere to the general civility code

As I mentioned earlier, the courts have stringent rules in order for one to claim hostile work environment. Rightfully, they see that most issues should be solved at the company level. Defense stated in their documents that I "ultimately seek to impose a general civility code upon employers..." Actually that was clearly my intent from the beginning-to place resolution in the hands of the organization rather than in the hands of the court. The company chose the latter to the extent of allowing the court's ruling to eradicate their obligation to address the situation at the organizational level.

Workplaces are not always harmonious locales. Incidents that cause bruises and wounds are worthy of the company taking the responsibility of having an open dialogue addressing these 'hurts' and seeking solutions. My experience has been that when people are remorseful of hurting someone, whether real or perceived and they are not 'guilty' of it, they profusely apologize in some way and make amends.

The actions of the company, all dressed in Non Mensch attire, continued to be done in reckless indifference to my wounds and bruises. Rather than trying to start salvaging the damaged pieces and mending the disconnection and fragmentation after the Summary Judgment verdict, the company chose to remain uninterested, uncaring, and unmoved. The CEO nor anyone else in the organization offered to talk with me about the best way to move forward. In fact just two days after the Judge's final ruling, my manager (HB) handed me my review of the entire previous year full of negativity and minutia. The Director of Support Services (KP) approved it. Three months later the manager 'wrote me up' with the strong approval of the Director of Support Services. This was the very first time in my 35+ years of being in the work environment that I was ever written up. Clearly the organization had no remorse. Clearly the company interpreted their being granted Summary Judgment as permission to continue their Non Mensch actions.

A Mensch organization would have worked harder to close the abscesses created by the lawsuit rather than exacerbate the situation.

Defense asked me in my deposition, "what if someone was offended by what you were doing, would you have stopped doing it?"

I know the answer is yes because I can relay two experiences I had where I not only stopped but also apologized.

- Back in the late 80's when I was working for the fortune 100 company, I said something to my co-worker from another country that I meant as a joke. He viewed it as a derogatory comment. He told our manager who immediately called me in to talk about it. When I realized my line was not taken in a humorous manner and I highly insulted someone, I sought him out immediately and apologized until I felt he knew I was authentic.

- Growing up in a tight Jewish community, I was not aware of many of the beliefs and values of Christian people. Yes, my community knew Christians believed in Jesus but it was just a sentence to us. We really were not aware of its strength. So we used the phrase "Jesus Christ" as an expletive no differently than we would say "Jiminy Crickets!" We meant no harm or blasphemy in using the former-it had no meaning to us other than a way to express ourselves emotionally.

That was about to change my freshman year away at college when my dorm roommate was a Catholic woman. Because using the phrase was routine and habit for me and never provided any consequences, I unconsciously kept saying it. Then one of my Jewish friends who roomed down the hall told me my roommate was probably uncomfortable with my saying that. I was astonished and told her she was most likely wrong but I said I would confirm with my roommate. You know the answer-yes, she did not appreciate my saying it and explained in more detail. I not only apologized but also have not used the term as such in almost a half century.

In neither of these situations did I ask anyone to take on my obligations. I responsibly addressed the people I injured face to face. Doing so is not a weakness but a strength.

CHAPTER 11

Acting Soon and Best

**"It takes two to tangle, but it takes only one to begin
the process of untangling a knotty situation."**
-William Ury, author of many books on negotiation

Now is a good time

DEFENSE PROFESSED SEVERAL times that the company was uninformed and blindsided (not their word) about my claim of discrimination and hostile work environment. It was their contention that the latter was revealed not until they were supplied the complaint as well as not until they requested my file from EEOC after we responded to their Motion to Dismiss. The contents of the file they received included my 5 page extended explanation which was attached to the EEOC intake questionnaire. They were concerned that neither I, the EEOC nor anyone else told them previously about these allegations.

As I mentioned earlier, I was green doing this so I took the advice of the EEOC agent. I had no intention of keeping it a secret.

Having said all this, I take exception to their querulous perception about not being told prior to litigation. They often referred to learning about the grievances as the first time. It doesn't matter when it was first disclosed. The time should not have offered any other action than to try to discuss it and remedy it immediately. Furthermore, at any given moment throughout the whole process, they could have stopped and asked that we discuss this together. It is always the right time to reduce if not eliminate any escalation of the issues and not let it get to litigation.

I did not talk much about the issue of discrimination because I felt I would be looked at differently for complaining about it. Evidence showed me I was constantly being judged as over reacting or too unreasonable. While I made the mistake of not very explicitly telling them I felt discriminated against because of my religion, I was very clear that many incidences that occurred were attacks on me and my beliefs.

At one point during the case my attorney said to me, "they aren't taking you seriously." No matter when I would have explicitly stated something, I am sure they would not have taken me seriously. They never did. They never showed they cared. Each and every time I mentioned something, they showed no concern in learning more and showed no attempt at making things better. It is my interpretation due to their behaviors that no matter when would have been the first time, they still would have done nothing.

- When I told the HR person about my manager telling me I was dead because I didn't reveal Jesus to me, she barely addressed it with the CEO. It was so unimportant to her that during discovery, she confused this episode that happened at the end of 2011 with an incident in spring of 2008. The latter was totally irrelevant to my case and insignificant to me.

Now is a good time to lead by accessing the compassionate, righteous, and humane part of you.

- When it was well known I was extremely uncomfortable at the holiday party 2011 because of the religious ambiance and Christian songs being sung, I was not queried more by the CEO, COO, or HR Director.

Now is a good time to lead by accessing the compassionate, righteous, and humane part of you.

- They were more concerned about people sending jokes and unrelated business conversations in email than they were about a manager who told a Jewish person, "you are dead because you don't reveal Jesus to you" or that the Jewish person was extremely uncomfortable at the mandated holiday party that had religious undertones and sang songs to include the phrase "Christ our Lord."

Now is a good time to lead by accessing the compassionate, righteous, and humane part of you.

- When the person in HR sent out an email that everyone was getting a Poinsettia for the holiday, I wrote her back to ask if I was getting a Menorah instead. She wrote back, "You're funny." I wasn't trying to be.

Now is a good time to lead by accessing the compassionate, righteous, and humane part of you.

I find it grossly absurd that the company acted the 'caught off guard' role that there would be a discrimination case filed against them. Even though I never mentioned discrimination, it should not have been lost on anyone at the organization. I would like to think each of the two CEO's mentioned in my complaint were intelligent enough to know there would be cause for a major intervention when an intelligent, skilled, and talented employee in a protected class is continually overlooked and rejected for advancement or a different role while so many others didn't suffer the same outcome.

Interestingly, the first CEO, RB, was obsessed with the law about sexual harassment and yet did not acknowledge its equivalence to religious harassment.

When a company's culture and philosophy are being characterized as anti-Semitic, it is time for leadership to take the situation seriously. Whether or not someone says the word discriminated (or any derivative), treat it as such and do your due diligence. Discrimination does not go away unless it is identified and confronted. No leader should wait for a situation to reach the high bar of legal discrimination to do something about it.

When the Board of Directors learned the company was embroiled in a discrimination lawsuit, it was time for them to take the situation seriously.

Officers of a Board of Directors are leaders-either Mensch or Non Mensch. I sent 3 officers of the Board of Directors an email after the close of my case requesting a meeting with them to inform them of the parts of the lawsuit they may not know and should know. They did not return my email. Mensch officers of a Mensch Board of Directors would have responded directly to the sender. It is the right and humane thing to do. The very least acceptable response would have stated, "We are forwarding your email to CM who can better help you on this." At the other end of the spectrum would have been a respectful and professional response something resembling, "yes, we will meet with you. Here are dates/times we have available."

Instead they forwarded my email to the CEO who then forwarded it to the HR person and the Director of Support Services, both of whom surprised me at my office to discuss with me. Want to be a Mensch?

Don't surprise your employees by just showing up. A Mensch respects each individual and that means they call first. It is a human courtesy.

Discrimination, a federal lawsuit, and a victimized employee are all serious matters.

Mediation

I was very sure the company would agree to mediation and would be wise enough to know creating a lawsuit would be an antithesis to any business models, philosophies or theories that advocate good management and organizational effectiveness.

I was surprised that the CEO rejected a mediation session. Some people offered their assessment of his decision as that typical of someone who thinks going to mediation would insinuate guilt. Ironically, refusing to mediate makes the guilt protrude. We all have a tendency to avoid what we fear so avoiding a face to face discussion allows that person to pretend the issue does not exist and consequently not have to admit any wrong doing. More importantly, there are truths that may have been exposed that he preferred keeping as lies.

It is sad to think that some organizations consider their strength to lie in being non-confrontational and in pursuing avoidance. Yet these actions usually are signs of cowardice and weakness. Non Mensch leaders rather be right than make things better.

To avoid confrontation, some find it easier to give the issue to someone else-such as a lawyer. Big mistake, huge (Yes, line in Pretty Woman). Know that by not confronting the situation you are encouraging the adversarial dynamics that pollute the atmosphere of the organization. As a leader, you are obligated to create collaborative alliances. Only a Non Mensch leader would exercise the former over the latter.

The EEOC agency was established for the very reason to try to avoid a lawsuit and to settle differences between the two parties long before embroiling the court system. The agency's value lies in giving the employer some warning about the conduct aggrieving the employee so that an opportunity can be made to resolve matters amicably without resorting to the courts.

Defense claimed they were not provided the warning or the opportunity to resolve matters amicably so litigation would be unnecessary. Yes they were warned-they received the charge. No matter how little or how much was stated on the initial charge they received, they were informed there was a discrimination issue. They were offered the chance to resolve the situation-they were offered free mediation when they received the charge.

EEOC and the Federal Court system both recommend using mediation. In fact, a very good majority of EEOC charges are resolved in the first 6 months not so much from their investigation but from the plaintiff and defendant meeting and coming to their own agreement. EEOC offers free conciliation in the event their investigation shows Title VII may have been violated. Conciliation is another attempt to settle differences without going through the legal process. I never fully grasped why defense submitted three documents to dismiss the case yet didn't care to try a method that would have terminated it quickly, reasonably and amiably.

I am very familiar with mediation and a huge advocate of it. I took 50 hours of instruction from the Attorney General's Office on mediation which culminated in a certificated designation and an opportunity to voluntarily mediate cases for them. The benefits of mediation cannot be ignored or minimized. Because of my lessons from the AG's office along with my extensive training in facilitation, I regularly use its concepts in my coaching business. Mediation which adopts a collaborative approach, produces positive results that cannot be reckoned with.

There is nothing more productive than hearing and reflecting on what the other person has to say. As a leader, the CEO missed the chance to solicit perceptions and address them and to build a back and forth dialogue. By creating a climate for favorable results, we could have reasoned through alternatives to turn a problem into possible solutions. The dialogue of mediation is forward moving.

There is no value to the organization for the case to go to litigation. Every lawsuit has a plaintiff (in some areas of law it is called petitioner) and a defendant (in some areas of law it is called the respondent). Having sides immediately conjures up the idea of positioning. People become entrenched in their positions and in their own point of view. Sticking to a position causes destructive and unproductive interactions. Walls get constructed limiting opportunities. Mediation allows people to go from an 'us/you' mindset to a 'we' mindset.

When you work from a lawsuit, you are continually rehashing over and over again the same past events. It is prudent of a leader to move forward and not stay stuck in the cement of the past. Mediation allows for open communication. Both parties will learn something-perceptions, interpretations, and beliefs, to name a few. In my case, there is much the CEO would have learned that he did not know or realize before.

At the initiation point of litigation, no one knows what the final ruling will be. The plaintiff will usually come out ahead if the court rules in her/his favor. However, there is no prize or reward for the defense if the results go in their direction. Much time, energy and money is wasted and misused.

My purpose for filing a charge was because I wanted a promotion or job change allowing me to use my education/experience in Organizational Behavior, Leadership development, team building, and coaching in order to provide more value to the company. My interest was not in holiday decorations or holiday parties. Unfortunately, the complaint and discovery focused way too much on these latter two-both eventually remedied while ignoring the real issue-job advancement/change. Had we mediated, we probably never would have discussed anything but my real issue.

The legal process made the case go off the beaten path. The main issue became more and more diluted the further we moved from it. Inaccurate information began to flourish. In my deposition, in their answers to interrogatories, and in Summary Judgement, the defense attorney continually made comments that denounced, ridiculed and condemned my religion, people and beliefs. Remember, he is representing the company. Litigation perpetuates the toxicity of the organization. It polarizes people rather than brings them together. Only a Non Mensch organization finds this attractive.

Always do what you can to not involve lawyers. It is always best for the parties involved in the conflict to resolve the issues together and not leave a verdict or ruling to the judge. In mediation, no third party dictates outcomes, actions or absolutes. A neutral third party who has no vested interest in the situation is there to facilitate the meeting of the parties and help direct its path. It is not mandated that anything gets finalized in mediation. It is for this reason alone that mediation is a viable choice. If it works, great. If not, there still is litigation-the option of a lawsuit is still on the table.

CHAPTER 12

The Mensch organization

The highest example is set by the leaders

DANCE 10, LOOKS 3 is a famous song in the musical *A Chorus Line*. The song tells the story of a woman who kept auditioning to dance on the Broadway stage and was continually rejected. She once had a peek at her dance card which read, Dance 10, Looks 3. She then saw what they were hiring. Her performance and talent were the tops but those who 'looked' great got the job. To meet the casting criteria, she had plastic surgery on two parts of her body. Per the song, she then got jobs readily.

I was 'dance 10' in job performance. Defense often stated I was never demoted or disciplined or issued a decrease in pay. Additionally the CEO (CM) testified I was intelligent and a talented trainer. In our conversations he told me he enjoyed our conversations adding that I was mentally sharp (a characteristic he claimed he likes in people), I was self-confident and successful. He never had a problem conversing with me using my intelligence and knowledge to solicit good information to move the company forward and into the future.

Yet I was not promoted, not given a different job title/function more specific to my knowledge, skills and abilities that go way beyond that

of training, and not given projects and responsibilities more in alignment with the contributions I could offer the company.

In 2009 I was asked to meet with the then CEO, RB, to discuss a
plan to enhance the performance of the staff members and the organization as a whole. I am very sure I was the only person who was
ever employed by this company (at least up to that time) to have
such knowledge and expertise in organizational design and development. I was well equipped to help make productive changes in
the organization. My proposal never got implemented and died a
quick death.

Mediocrity is often a good choice for Non Mensch leaders who may
be threatened or intimidated by dance 10. I saw what they were
approving in management. I was obviously 'looks 3' in not enough
incompetence for management. Using the song as my inspiration, I
submitted a list of behaviors the company could expect me to start
doing now noting nonproductive behaviors of my manager.

I wrote I had to start saying "well, that's the way it is" to be unrecep-
tive to other's comments and I had to give someone else anything
I did not want to do. I wrote my list up and submitted it to the HR
Director. Apparently no one in senior leadership saw *A Chorus Line*.
They were not taken in by the changes I was anticipating doing. Of
course my list should have been taken as it was delivered-tongue in
cheek. They included this in their Summary Judgment stating that it is
not up to me determine what job duties I would perform.

I did precede my list by saying the manager's behaviors go above
reproach so I assume what she does is encouraged and approved.
Therefore, she is walking the talk of the organization so I will start
emulating her actions. The company severely missed the mark.
Perhaps they were unaware that managers are supposed to model
the behaviors they want from others. A Mensch leadership would see

the importance of my statements illustrating poor management that employees should not be emulating. They would see it as a great feedback moment for the company to start making some corrections that would promote high performing management behaviors. Instead, they chastised me and submitted the document in Summary Judgment as their evidence of my "boorish" behavior.

Looking through transparency

For some organizations that boast transparency, the only thing they are transparent about is their lack of transparency. Experiences I had highlighted areas where a company needs to be transparent.

- Employees should always be informed of the purpose for their work. I was the lead in a project that entailed using affiliates to help us train our subscribers. The manager, HB, asked me to do a task regarding this project that seemed senseless and wasteful. I was sure there was nothing she was going to do with the stats she asked me to track.

It was clear the Board members were not necessarily pleased with this affiliate partnering even though it proved successful. I was curious as to why I was being asked to do this task and assumed it was because the Board members were requesting it. So I inquired of her, "why?" Her response was, "because I want it and that is all you need to know."

Most other times when she was asked to let me and/or the department members know the reasoning for a directive from her, she would respond staunchly, "I am the manager."

When a manager responds as such, they are working from the 1% card; they are falling back on their title and their perceived power and formal authority of it. It is when managers rely on the 99%-when they are unafraid to give clear explanations for their decisions and directives that the manager is worthy of respect and the more important title of Mensch. Those who work from the 99% card of what they do never need to remind others of their title or position. People are more apt to respect the 99% and not the 1%.

- Employees should always be informed of the meaning and purpose underlying actions and decisions made concerning them.

I never hid my desire to have another position with the company. In 2008 I applied for the support services manager (immediately title changed to Director) and thought for sure I would be granted the position since I was extremely well qualified and the CEO, RB, said that everything being equal, positions would be granted to internal candidates first. The position was accepted by an outside candidate who became my manager for the next eight years. The CEO denied HB and I were 'unequal' although I informed him that my having a Master of Arts in Organizational Behavior/Design with a strong concentration in training and development as well as experience as a High School English teacher far exceeded the incoming manager who had a high school diploma and no education at all in training.

Later in 2008 I asked the CEO to divide the support department into help desk and training and to give the training side to me while the manager hired earlier would take the support side. He laughed saying the combined departments was not an overload of responsibilities. Yet a year later he brought on board CM and did indeed separate the two functions and gave CM the position of Director of Support Services and the manager who up until then had this title/position was going to be Training Manager.

No one in management at the company ever gave me a reason why I was never promoted, or why others less qualified than I were either promoted or assigned a different title offering different tasks and responsibilities.

The company was very hard pressed to present negative information about me in the discovery phase of the litigation. My employee file contained great reviews on me, wonderful statements from people in my classes who responded to the feedback questionnaire, and emails that suggested my advanced thinking skills, my efficient human relations skills, and my high level communication skills. The very worst item in my file was the questionable anonymous letter which still remains inconclusive about who did indeed write it.

Since I was never given a reason for the choices to which they subjected me, I interpret their silence to be hiding a reality that for them seemed best to keep buried.

Between the end of 2012 and the beginning of 2013 I had several meetings with the CEO, CM when I asked him to give me a position to do staff development/employee relations, trade out the current training manager and me, or at minimum to change my title and responsibilities. To help him out for either trading me out with the manager or changing my job title and responsibilities, I supplied him with many training job titles and descriptions from online postings from other companies.

In these meetings, we never spoke about any other positions than staff development and training manager. It wasn't until the interrogatories during the discovery phase of litigation that I was asked to present a list of every employment position I should have been afforded. I obliged and offered 4 different positions for which I reasonably could have been considered-which is not the same as should have been placed. These included Director of Support Operations; Director of Education and Staff Development; Director of Communications, Business & Professional Development; Support Services Director.

My request for a job change became an issue in the lawsuit. When I was deposed, I was asked about all of these positions and why I felt qualified. Here is the first area for a discussion on transparency. The job descriptions and minimum qualifications for these positions were never made available for all to see. You know, the chicken thing- were the descriptions determined before the position was filled or was the positioned filled before the description?

Transparency means each job position has a written job description with its qualifications available for viewing by all in the company- before the position is filled. When they are visible:

- Employees know what positions are in the company for which they may want to prepare

- Employees know what to expect of each position and if necessary, help others be accountable

The question posed by defense was perplexing. Without having this information available to me, I was unable to align my answer with the job description. I gave my answer as I viewed how the people in those positions performed. This made it easy for me to declare why I was qualified since I was sure I could have performed the job function of each expertly. Regarding the position of Director of Support Services, defense wrote in Summary Judgment, "…she acknowledges that she doesn't know what this position entails." Of course I didn't. The company was not transparent.

Defense went on to say in Summary Judgment that I did not know the qualifications of the person in that position. That statement is illogical. When people apply for jobs for which they are not currently working, they don't know the qualifications of others going for the same position. They only know their own qualifications. With that in mind, I knew I was qualified which warranted my being considered.

Again illogic prevailed when they used in their defense that this last position wasn't posted. My covert response to that: "So what?" 'Nuff' said.

Let's go back to the idea of transparency and look at these facts.

Remember I gave the CEO, CM, postings of jobs from other companies? Well, at a follow up meeting he and I had, he told me he still had them but hadn't looked at them.

At these meetings when I asked for a change in position he said there were no vacancies yet he created positions or placed people in positions.

At these meetings he told me he needed board approval for adding positions. Yet, he never asked the board to approve a new position for me.

I asked him if the company grew, would he consider me for another position. He declared NO.

When I offered the viable option to divide the HR department into employee relations-for which I was well qualified and Benefits/ Compensation for which the current HR Director was an expert, the answer was just NO.

The issue was not if I were more or less qualified than others; it was simply the CEO was not going to give me another position or job function. Shortly after I filed my charge with EEOC, the CEO redesigned the organizational chart. Still, my name and function stayed in the same box.

I was deliberately being kept stuck where I was and kept reporting to whom I was reporting. Several times in the meetings I had with the

CEO to discuss issues in the organization, he referenced his desire for me to leave the company. For example he once said, "If you are unhappy, well, I would hate to see you leave but…" I never said I was unhappy nor that I wanted to leave so he conveniently mistook my making suggestions for being unhappy and wanting to leave.

Rather than being transparent and authentic, the CEO hid behind the twists his attorney created for why I did not get other positions.

The organizational chart

The traditional hierarchal organizational chart is a pyramid with power at the top. It is not a diagram of respect. The people at the top of the chart are due no more respect than the people at the bottom level. This chart also creates silos and barriers between departments. The traditional chart should be used solely to show a design of the organization much like blueprints for building a house.

An organization is a structure of relationships – interdependent parts sharing the same goal. It is important that each person-vertically and horizontally on the organizational chart lets all know the following: how s/he looks at own department, what her goals are, how she works, and what she expects of herself and what she needs from each and where she is in the chain of internal customer/supplier. Make job descriptions visible. It is wise for staff members to understand the strengths, values, proposed contribution, and working style of those with whom they work and on whom they depend in order to make use of these.

"I must follow the people. Am I not their leader?"
-British Prime Minister Benjamin Disraeli,
19th century.

Consider these ways to shake up the traditional organizational chart.

Invert the chart so that it shows the employees are at the top. As a leader, you serve and work for your employees.

Stop being controlled by the boxes on the chart. To increase the quality of the vertical and horizontal relationships, switch it around.

Make it circular. I call this the round table. This shows everyone in the organization is equal. Not all leaders are in a leadership position.

Make it one horizontal or vertical line and keep changing the location of the individuals.

Make the chart more human. Add pictures of the people. Here is a good place for some transparency. Write a brief description of the role of each title on the chart.

Each person in the organization is a link in the chain directing them to the external customer. All employees need to be aware of their output on which others in the company rely as well as know those in the company on whom they rely to do their job. Creativity, productivity and motivation increase when people see their interconnectivity. Too many times there is a lack of consistency of efforts intra-departmentally as well as inter-departmentally which causes rework, frustration and conflict. We often forget that we need to service our internal customers with fairness, benevolence, and accuracy.

Policy and Procedure handbook

Most organizations have a Policy and Procedure handbook often created from a template and tweaked where needed. The handbook is a great guide to be sure everyone is on the same page (no pun intended). The handbook should be consistent and flexible and be void of roadblocks to empower employees. The policies should be valuable and necessary so they are not frustrating or easily broken.

Problems can occur when…

- The policy has too much room for interpretation

Too much attention was placed on my 'violating' the policy on using company email for personal use. The policy first states that using the company email for personal use should not interfere with job duties, performance or company operations. When I sent my email about Chanukah, I was not guilty of any of those things. The policy continues to be specific on what the emails cannot include such as pornography or company trade secrets. Again my email was neither of those. The email I sent to staff was educational. The subject line was "another seasonal holiday" and was a copy and paste that anyone could have done-it was not written in first person. It was sent in response to the highly religious holiday party we had. My email was not propaganda or solicitation trying to convert anyone. It was merely a historic account of a holiday.

In my deposition I stated my email was not personal because it was nothing personal about me. Additionally, it was not personal use since I was not writing to a friend outside of the company. Loopholes and room for interpretations exist not only in company employee handbooks but also in law as well as our constitution. In both of these last two, both sides of an issue get to be heard. Therefore, defense was stifling this privilege we have by stating in the Summary Judgment that instead of arguing my point, I should have acknowledged I violated the policy and move on.

- Policies are limited in scope

Diversity, while it looks nice as a topic in the employee handbook, is only valuable when it is clearly implemented. It is the obligation of the organization to be sure each person is understood and respected for their individuality. A mandated online class on diversity and harassment is nothing more than veneer. It is knowing about others that matters. My situation with the email about Chanukah has more components than just the company insisting I violated policy. It should not be acceptable to use the policy of emails to eliminate celebrating holidays other than Christmas. The email told the history of the holiday and had nothing religious in it. Sending this information was a great way of correcting the error of my manager who wrote in an email to staff that Chanukah was the celebration of lighting candles. For the record, there is not a Jewish holiday that celebrates the act of lighting candles. As usual, during my deposition defense asked if I was offended by the definition of Chanukah by my manager. No, I was not-I just want people to know the truth. Chanukah is the celebration of the rededication of the Second Temple in Jerusalem. I am sure if I said Christmas was the celebration of three wise men who went to see a new baby, I would be corrected. Defense continued on this same topic to ask if I would be offended if a Christian person said Christmas was the celebration of the birth of Jesus. Even though I was hoping he was being facetious, I still answered. "Why would I be offended? That is the purpose of Christmas." If anyone asked me what does Christmas celebrate, I would respond, "the birth of Jesus."

It is the short sightedness of a Non Mensch leadership that values this hypocrisy of the email and holiday party more than they value diversity and learning. Usually the root cause of a strong prejudice is ignorance-not knowing. We all have a responsibility to overturn bigotry so when an opportunity presents itself to educate-well, even companies need to take heed. Additionally, the email could have been a valuable springboard to work with staff to reach *Mensch* status. I supplied a link in the email that went to a site talking about the miracles of Chanukah. Interestingly, they go beyond the miracle of the extended use of the oil. The miracles describe the miracles in each of us.

» Victory of the few against the many

- » The courage to be different

- » Taking risks and chances-taking a leap of faith

- Procedures are not followed when warranted

The Employee handbook for this company stated that if you have a complaint or are bothered by a job-related situation, you should first speak to your manager. That is exactly what I did concerning the problem I had with the religiously based holiday party of 2011. Yet in my deposition, defense badgered me asking, "Why didn't you go to the HR Director after the holiday party to complain about this? You weren't intending to go to her to complain about it, were you?" I also testified that my manager spoke to me about this because she was advised from her manager who was a director. The HR Director testified she knew about my take on the party. Senior leadership was also aware so there was no need for me to go to the HR Director. As long as they knew, my job of advising was done. It would be redundant to 'complain.' Besides, my manager, as a leader, gave the response for all -"interesting." And once they knew, no one did anything. Their inactivity in regards to speaking with me should have been questioned more than my intentions.

- The handbook also addressed the investigation procedure for the policy of prohibited harassment. It was written that when the company receives a complaint, "an appropriate and unbiased investigation will be conducted as quickly as practical." A determination will be made after the investigation to include the findings and proposed remedy as appropriate. "In all cases, the complainant will be informed of the determination...the determination will be reviewed and discussed with the complainant by the investigator and/or CEO."

The statement in the policy seems very clear and yet not enforced. I complained to the HR Director about the manager making the comment about my being dead…I was never informed about the determination of the investigation-ever. Per the policy, no matter what, the CEO was supposed to advise me of the determination. Neither the HR Director nor the CEO, RB, talked to me about this issue after I made my complaint. Because I was never advised of the findings and/or remedy and because the HR person testified (falsely) she did not know about the statement until the lawsuit, I can only surmise she dropped the ball and did not do what was expected of her per the policy.

In his deposition, the CEO, CM, was asked hypothetically what he would do about following up on a complaint from an employee equivalent to my issue. He testified he would ask the HR person but not the employee if it had been remedied and resolved. First, this is not what the policy dictates and second, not asking the injured party about resolution is the highest form of insult-more than the issue itself. A Mensch leader would show respect and ask the employee if s/he finds the issue remedied and resolved.

- Shortly after the close of my case, my manager 'wrote me up' substantiating it with a reference to the Employee Handbook under disciplinary action. She claimed I violated an item "to complete assignments and projects on time." Yet, this is not an item on the list of approximately 33 items offering "examples of misconduct that will lead to disciplinary action (up to and including discharge of employees). However, one of those items states, "making insensitive or improper remarks to anyone concerning one's religion…or other protected characteristics." Another item in the handbook stated a definition of harassment to be "verbal conduct…insulting or offensive words…based on or relating to…religion…" She was not written up or even reprimanded (per the sworn testimonial from HB) for telling me I was dead because I did not reveal

Jesus to me or that she assisted planning the very religious party to include carolers singing songs referencing religious belief systems.

- There is an absence of important policies

While there was a policy about using company equipment, there was a blatant absence of a policy about using company facility for religious functions. It is because of such that my email about Chanukah was a topic of condemnation and a mandated religiously Christian holiday party at the company facility was allowed. A Mensch leader in an altruistic environment would look at the big picture and recognize that a mandated religiously Christian holiday party is far from business related and much more serious than an email educating on a holiday.

When a party is on company time and location and mandated, it should not be religious in ambiance and song. However, if the company decides to go forward with this type of party, staff should be warned and able to choose to attend or not without any repercussions. It would be prudent to have such a policy. While I may be taking some liberties in my interpretation, it is still worthy to note that EEOC states that an employee cannot be forced to participate (or not participate) in a religious activity as a condition of employment.

Open door policy

In its response to my EEOC charge, defense stated, "Despite (company) open door policy…"

The company had no open door policy-at least no policy was mentioned in the employee handbook.

Many companies act as if they have such a policy by giving it lip service. Unless a company has a specific system for the policy, open door policies are non-existent. The term is overused and used incorrectly.

The fortune 100 international company with whom I was employed many years ago had a detailed process and program in place for employees to express their grievances and for management to respond responsibly. They were an extremely large organization so their process followed a chain of command. When a company does not explicitly delineate the steps for their open door stand, nothing more than a 'willy nilly' procedure takes place. Every open door policy should have written standards of procedure which usually are part of the handbook.

The purpose of an open door policy is to encourage positive open communication, feedback and discussion. This information very often could be used to make changes or improvements in the organization. (And let's face it, it is much more reasonable to make needed enhancements at this point than to wait for litigation to do so). An open door policy needs to mean that when a person comes to talk to a manager, they are assured a safe place to speak and express their hopes, dreams, issues, needs, wants, concerns, hurts and pains. It also means that the manager listens and not use the time to destroy the speaker.

An open door policy provides a vehicle for senior leadership to understand what is on the minds of employees with whom they don't regularly interact. The policy is a message from management to employees saying, "My door is always open for you to discuss concerns, ask questions, and make suggestions."

The policy should also make it clear that no retaliation will occur from any topic brought to the table.

After one of my performance reviews from my manager, I wrote a detailed response to it and asked her manager, the Director of Support Services, if he would like to meet so he could be apprised of the response's content. He declined meeting and then added, "However, as always, my door is open if you wish to meet…"

This is a mixed message-not much different from a client of mine who told me she was on a first date with a gentleman. As they were parting for the night she asked him if she would see him again to which he replied, "I don't see why not." Then proceeded to say, "Take care." FYI: in the dating world, that means "No, you will not see me again."

I may have deviated from the idea of open door policy but the message I have for everyone who chooses Mensch over Non Mensch -company or individual is: Say what you mean and mean what you say.

Another time I went to speak to this same person to let him know my manager was accusing me of not doing a task due within 7 days which I indeed completed on time. The Director was ornery and treated me rudely and indignantly from the beginning of our meeting to the end. The end only came because I finally walked out.

On the bright side, there were a couple of times this same Director did treat the concept of open door policy with dignity and respect. He listened to me, inquired to get the details, and let me know the next steps he was going to take. He did send me his notes on the meeting for me to review and add/correct if necessary and then he got back with me with the results.

And that is how it should be done.

CHAPTER 13

Humanizing the workplace

Speaking employees should not be quieted

WHEN COMPANIES LOOK at their costs, usually the highest one is employees' salaries. It would seem logical that if your employees are your biggest expense, they are probably your biggest asset. Yet, too many companies miss the mark and pay out much money while not getting a full return on their investment. No, I don't mean overwork the employees with menial tasks. That worked well when we were in an industrial economy long ago and workers were merely expected to put widget A in slot widget B. Today we are in a knowledge economy. It is the combination of knowledge that matters and not the sameness of how you do things. The difference between making a mediocre company soar and sabotaging an outstanding one is choosing to listen to your staff or ignore their valuable input. If you are one of those companies, usually ego driven, which claims only those in a management position have the right to be heard, you better have the most intelligent people in the world occupying those roles.

Mensch companies know all people in the organization should be tapped for their aptitude. The fortune 100 company for which I worked previously, had a reward program for implemented suggestions received from employees at all levels of the organization. In fact, it was expected for employees to spot areas that should be questioned and improved. A Mensch company values employee involvement and never stymies employees from speaking their thoughts and opinions. They unleash the ideas, energy and enthusiastic efforts of all. Managers and senior leaders who discourage such are only sending a signal they are too afraid to admit their position does not equal all knowing. Mensch companies ensure each person's uniqueness is respected and allowed expression.

> **"To impede communication is to reduce people to the status of things"**
>
> – Freire, a world educator.

At one of our department meetings a manager from another department came to speak to us about a security system being put in place that utilized a video camera. This action was in response to an episode I had prior to that in which I was rattled by a stranger who started a conversation with me as I was entering my office location. I suggested to the CEO afterward that better than a video camera (or in addition to) at some locations, a panic button might be best. Now I was learning that their agenda proposed to install a video camera only. I spoke my concerns about safety saying the camera would be good to see who 'did' the crime-past tense- but not help prevent the crime as a panic button may be able to do. It was a good conversation that was void of any argument or belligerence. Even still, my manager wrote on my review that I should stop "questioning in public with other employees policies or procedures that are announced" and I need to stop talking to fellow employees about issues that need to be changed at the company. I brought this issue to her manager, the Director of Support Services and informed him that with a bit of stretching, it may violate sections 7 and 8 of the National Labor Relations Act (NLRA).

Whether or not this episode violates a legality, it is far from good business practice. Having a good discussion about security (or any topic you have) with staff members at all levels of the organization affords the company an opportunity to brainstorm best options and solutions.

My main role at the fortune 100 company with whom I was employed prior to this company was to work with 'problem solving' teams (known as Quality Action Teams). The company had a process in place that was conducive to getting good results for the company through the synergy of the many.

Problem solving is not privilege for some; it is an obligation of everyone.

A primary part of my coaching business is group coaching or interactive webinars. Why? Simple. I know that alone I am greatly reduced in my capacity to serve any vision larger than myself. I also know there is wisdom in each of us that is separate from all others. We need everyone's wisdom for the wisest results. We learn from exploring other's experiences, values and knowledge.

The great writer and philosopher Voltaire once said, "Judge a man by his questions rather than his answers."

Look for the true, the good and the possible. Change happens with the first question asked.

There is no reason why an organization should not welcome challenges of the paradigms and assumptions that exist in the organization. My manager, personally bothered by my speaking up, wrote on my reviews:

"Only after a lot of arguing at times will Marcy accept decisions that have been made. It creates a difficult work environment." She continued to state improvement requires my "accepting the changes in the company and supporting the decisions."

"Marcy challenges the intentions of the company when new policies are initiated instead of supporting the goals and values."

While both of these comments were over exaggerated, they do both say the truth that I did sometimes question why or I would share concerns of the feasibility and logic of the decisions. I always spoke to help the organization and not to ridicule it. The manager considered my asking questions to be aggression so she would respond defensively.

Asking about the policies is not the same as offering no support. If the organization perceives being challenged as a lack of support-well, all the more reason to listen. And the best way to listen is to include employees in the decision making process. The secret has been out for quite some time: people buy in to that which they help create.

If staff acquiesces because they act out of intimidation, no one has succeeded in inspiring commitment or an approachable organization. People rarely are committed to a solution if they have no input into it. People work best when they know how and why decisions are made, feel part of the decision making process and see their direct influence on successes. When organizations perform this way, they paint a picture of mutual success.

People who are willing to challenge you will ultimately make you look good. 'Yes people' do not. They may make you feel good briefly, but in the long run, they will take you down and shatter an organization.

Organizations should encourage and expect collective thinking from all its members. It does not matter at what level an idea comes. Non Mensch organizations develop strategies that deliberately take thinking out of the mix. Mensch leaders combine the qualities of all staff to achieve results. Organizations invest much in their employees so they need to reap its benefits by listening to their ideas.

A leader must encourage an active, continuing communication of concerns, obstacles, insights and suggestions from employees. Always listen to the voice of your employees. While all people may not be wise, all have wisdom. People come with experiences, knowledge, communities, and cultures that allow them to bring ideas, innovations, and strategies. You get a group of passive-aggressive employees when you quiet them. Don't lobotomize your employees.

In a meeting I had with the CEO, I began to tell him my grievances with my manager. He clearly told me I did not get to talk about that.

Colin Powell is reputed to have taken strolls so people could vent. He advised: the day soldiers stop bringing you their problems, is the day you have stopped leading them. They have either lost confidence that you can help them or concluded you do not care. Either case is a failure of leadership.

Employees need to speak

Of course, leaders can only listen when people speak. Often an employee would tell me a concern s/he had with a person in the company or the company as a whole. I would advise them to tell their manager. "Oh no," they would respond. "I don't want to make waves or get in trouble." Then I would give them the advice I got from my manager at the fortune 100 company for which I worked, "If you don't like what is happening, either do something about it or shut up!" I have personally lived by that statement for nearly thirty years (hence, my legal charge and complaint of discrimination).

For each of you who has something to say (and you all do), speak. Stand up for your beliefs and your dreams. Question the rules and policies blessed by top brass. If they tried to silence me, I spoke louder.

You always have the right to not only be treated the way you want, but to let people know when their actions are in direct opposition.

Don't put up with behaviors that you don't like- no matter your level on the organizational chart.

My manager sent me an email that I found to be very sarcastic so I wrote her back telling her so. She merely wrote back it wasn't meant to be. I was hardly convinced since she did not offer an alternative statement. I then offered to work with her to find ways she could have said that differently so I would not find it sarcastic. She did not respond although several months later her manager, the Director of Support Services, met with me and asked the question to which I had become accustomed from my deposition, "is that the way to speak to a manager?" Emphatically I said, "Yes." I was speaking to another human being and being human always supersedes being a manager. I told him I was not speaking for anyone else. I was not telling her how to do her job. I was telling her I did not like how she was treating me and yes, I get to tell people how I want to be treated. No one has the right to demean or insult or bully anyone no matter what their title is. I continued to tell him, "I am the only person who gets to determine how I am treated. No one else gets to determine that." He did not disagree at all.

There is a difference between telling a manager how to do his/her job and giving a suggestion so they can better themselves as a human being. No manager is doused in fairy dust allowing them to fly above all others. We all have the responsibility to start the process of helping each person become a Mensch and each of us has the responsibility of accepting help to become a Mensch.

Don't be shy about offering suggestions to improve the quality and scope of work at your company, even if your opinions are neither solicited nor encouraged. Companies can't afford to dismiss valuable ideas.

The key is to communicate authentically using effective communication skills. Start by owning your perceptions and feelings. Authentic communication means you relay information directly, clearly, honestly and objectively about what you observe, think, feel, like, dislike, want or need. It is void of attacking, judging, controlling or threatening.

A good way to do this is to use "I" messages which helps place the responsibility on the speaker. Remember, it is the speaker who has the issue. "I" messages are useful when giving criticism, explaining a problem, making a suggestion, or expressing an opinion. They help us focus on aspects of a situation that we can control.

The "I" message usually looks like this: I feel (disappointed, hurt...) when you (insert behavior of other person) because (the effect). What I would like is for you to (request). Notice how using this method lowers the level of conflict and reduces antagonism by having the speaker take ownership of feelings, giving a reason and then making a request and not a demand.

If I had taken my own advice, I could have said the following to the CEO: I feel discriminated against when you ignore my requests for a different job title, role, function, position and offer any or all to many others. What I would like is for you to not only acknowledge my intelligence and skills verbally, but to act on them.

It is not only presumptuous to consider the person to whom one reports is the only one in the world who has all the skills and knowledge to help another evolve but also a huge burden on the person delivering the content. Helping anyone be a Mensch is the obligation of us all.

People need to hear your voice. Don't deprive the world of hearing from you.

Reviews, Rewards, and Recognitions

Most organizations have a formal employee review process that usually takes place a minimum of once a year. Two problems often occur. The first is the form that is used often is poorly conceived as well as wrongly filled out. The other problem is that most managers lack the skills and training needed to make reviews beneficial for the company.

The review forms my company used had a total of 18 sub categories that were measured with an "A" for above expectations, "M" meets expectations, and "U" for unacceptable. While each had a two sentence generic definition, none of the 18 sub categories was defined or assigned specific actions. It is crucial that reviews remain extremely objective. Usually the attempt of a manager to substantiate her evaluation is nothing more than a subjective opinion dressed in an outer layer of minutia. A good way to prevent such subjectivity is to determine the desired level of performance of each sub category. Then see how the actual or current level of performance meets the desired level. If there is a gap, do an analysis to determine what is causing the gap. Take steps needed to close the gap, measure the results, and take additional action if needed.

Too many reviews are driven by finding deficits no matter how small they are. It is important that reviews present no surprises. Managers should not wait until the review to list all the negative minutia they have been storing. It is also imperative that the person who signs off on the review, in my case the Director, discusses with the manager what would make the review more effective and less emotional.

My reviews that were once positive ceased to be so once I filed the charge with EEOC. Needless to say, that was no coincidence but a cause and effect. My manager, like others I am sure, used the review process to use her perceived power to retaliate (not per the legal definition). When once I was getting one or two checkmarks in the A column and none in the U column, I was now getting no checkmarks in the A column and at least 2 in the U column.

Reviews are meant to generate value from the employee to the organization. Reviews should always be attached to the goals of the organization. The indices and goals of the organization need to be powerful enough to encourage forward movement yet simple enough that each employee can embrace them. Put the company's goals foremost in your employees' minds and measure them based on how much their actions move those goals forward. When everyone is clear what the goals and indices are and what they need to do to contribute to them, the manager has no other choice than to be objective and to let go of the negative emotions directing them down the unproductive path. Reviews need to be used so employees are motivated to top organizational goals and not topple them.

Reviews are a time for dialogue. Just two days after the Judge's final ruling on my lawsuit, my manager presented me with my review for the previous year-yes, an entire year. She check marked no boxes indicating above expectations (A) and check marked 2 boxes referring to unacceptable (U). I voiced my concern that I was given no 'above' and two 'under.' Her response to why such an imbalance, was "sorry." Only saying "sorry" is a monologue and there is no place for such when a legitimate concern is presented.

Reviews should show forward thinking and focus on what the person can do to grow even more. Those who give reviews need to try and stay away from what the reviewee did not do. It is usually of little benefit to elaborate on what was not done. It is history and we can't go back and change it. Give more attention to what they did do.

In one of my reviews, the manager wrote I did not respond to emails from subscribers within the 24 hour time period she required. I wrote in my response that I did respond within 24 hours to 60 emails which is a much larger number than 2. I answered the emails timely 97% of the time.

The review should incorporate John Gottman's (a famous psychological researcher and clinician) idea of giving 5 appreciations for each negative response. Using Gottman's suggestion of 5 to 1 ratio of positive to negative comments, the manager could have made my answering 97% of the calls timely as the focal point rather than the 3%. The 3% could have been addressed as long as the 97% was the topic.

Refrain from being picayune in the review. In fact, a good idea is to use the legal description of hostile work environment (tweaked a bit) when including negative behaviors: the action needs to be severe-not just obnoxious but severe to create damage. Case law sited in my lawsuit documentation said courts should not consider each incident...in isolation. Rather a court must evaluate the sum total... over time. Reviews should not just pick out one small item if it is in isolation. The behavior needs to be pervasive and routine. One example is not enough to justify a negative response on the review.

Non Mensch managers will focus on an isolated item to satisfy their own anger. If you are that angry, punch a pillow but don't belittle another person. A manager is first and foremost a human being and as such, this person does not have the right to ridicule another for their own satisfaction.

Every organization needs to have a culture that promotes rewarding and recognizing all employees in a positive way. It is not hard to do. The problem as David Cooperrider, the recognized co-founder of the theory of Appreciative Inquiry, states is that we are so inculcated in the language of deficit that it is hard to see appreciative opportunities. Appreciative Inquiry, using the 'appreciative eye,' focuses on what is abundant and inspiring rather than on the problematic and the deficit. If you want a real shift in someone's performance, start working on using positive language. Every time you begin to say something negative, stop and consider 5 positive words or phrases you can use instead.

Showing appreciation needs to be a part of the business model. Acknowledge people for accomplishments or achievements no matter how small they are. The company for which I worked celebrated "employee appreciation week" by doing specific activities and presenting gifts almost daily to each employee. One year my manager gave me a letter of the top 10 things she appreciated about me. Initially I was touched and flattered. I reviewed the list again and noticed one item on there was not indicative of any quality I had or action I did. I soon found out that not only did she give the same list to all the members of the department, she also took it from her search on the Internet. I am not sure if this proved her more to be insincere and uncaring or simply not intelligent enough to come up with a list of her own specific items for each person. Giving praise for individual accomplishments shows you are paying attention. Don't underestimate the power of a kudo, a pat on the back, or a high five. When you celebrate accomplishments and victories, you will then ensure the vitality, heart and soul of the organization.

While few people might like tangible rewards such as money, most enjoy rewards that are of the spirit and heart. Whether as an employee or any other role one plays in life, each person likes to receive accolades their way. It is important in the workplace for managers to have a handle on what makes staff members feel good and what are their most motivational factors.

A Mensch manager lets people know they and their work are valued.

Dialogue and conversation- the only way to communicate

Mensch organizations have leaders who communicate dynamically.

In my deposition, defense asked 'why' questions a minimum of 16 times. The most repeated question was why I didn't go to the HR Director and tell about comments that were made when I was upset. There is one universal reason- when the issue initially occurs it may seem insignificant. I suppose if we all had a crystal ball to see its importance down the road, we would raise these issues continually. On a personal level, I did not go to the HR Director because when I did nothing got done, it was used against me, or the person in the HR position was unskilled at dealing with these issues. If you want your HR department to be the go-to source for communication, then you better have your HR department to be a good avenue of communication.

After the episode when my manager refused to give me a reason for the senseless task she was giving me, I told the CEO, CM, who told me to bring it to the HR Director which I then did. She proceeded to speak in private with the manager about my complaint and then decided to have a meeting with the three of us. I agreed making the assumption that the HR person would act as the mediator. It turned out she continually ridiculed me in front of the manager and did not try to resolve the issue at all. When she and I were alone, I told her that no person should ever feel as lousy (my own transparency here-I actually used another word) as I was feeling. I then proceeded to give her some tips about mediation that I learned from my classes at the Attorney General's office. She was momentarily responsive and perhaps even appreciative for my help. I never saw it go further though.

Now add to that experience to her dropping the ball on investigating the situation with the manager saying I was dead because I did not reveal Jesus to me, her lying under oath, and her taking the written document she requested of my summarizing our meeting in May 2015 and including it in my lawsuit to defame my character and I cannot imagine why anyone would question my lack of desire to go to the HR Director when I was upset.

Immediately after the close of my case, my manager had me in her office to go over my review of the previous year. The results of the review and her verbal comments were nothing short of retaliatory behaviors on her part. She used the opportunity –and her perceived power-to let me know she was not going to leave the lawsuit behind.

Since the employee handbook had a topic called Retaliation Prohibited that stated *the company would not tolerate or allow any form of reprisal by anyone against an employee who has made a (discrimination) complaint… and if an employee believes s/he has been retaliated against because of making a complaint must report it immediately to HR, the Director of the department or the CEO*, I was going to be smart this time and adhere to the process. I immediately went to the HR department (now headed by VJ with the title of HR Business Partner) to discuss the issue of retaliation. I made sure the company knew about it so they would not be blindsided as they insisted they were about my EEOC charge. On the downside, the HR department seemed to learn nothing from the lawsuit proceedings. On the upside, I was totally vindicated. The response of the HR person, VJ, was anything but professional or appropriate. His handling of the situation in our discussion proved to me that had I told senior leadership prior to my filing with EEOC that I felt discriminated against, nothing would have been investigated or resolved.

I began my conversation with him advising why I considered my review to be a sign of retaliation and at minimum extremely subjective, biased, and pathetically delivered. His behaviors confirmed why defense had to continually ask me why I did not go to the HR department and complain. There was no value to my talking to the

HR person whether it be the original person in that position or her replacement. Neither had the skills of a Mensch HR person. VJ spoke in platitudes. He did not inquire at all-just gave his textbook statements. I found myself going through a maze of foolishness and nonsense. As soon as I realized I could soon be trapped, I told him we were getting nowhere with his comments and attitude so I dismissed myself from the meeting. His gibberish response only solidified my contention I had that the company missed the mark in not using my talents, skills, and qualities to boost effectiveness in people interactions.

Had the CEO put me in a position of staff development, this HR person, VJ, would have been coached and educated to totally focus on the person in front of him and make it safe for the person to be vulnerable. When people sense we are receptive to their ideas and feelings, they feel safe to open up.

Stay with the person and their issue. Instead of focusing on me, VJ immediately diverted his attention to the manager saying he did not know what her goals and expectations were. The conversation remained in that corner. When someone comes to talk to you about a problem or issue, work with the person in front of you. S/he and not the problem they are facing is the subject and topic. There is an amazing person in front of you. Get a good handle on what this person wants during the time with you.

Inquire. Be more interested than interesting. Be *other* centered. Be present. When someone comes to you with their issue, your job is just to hear what is being said. Listen as if this is the most interesting thing you have ever heard. Listen to understand without providing an immediate response or reaction. Encourage the person in front of you to explore it fully – their meanings, beliefs, feelings, wants, and needs-by making comments such as, "I would like to hear more about this" or "tell me more." Pretend you are able to double click to open up a dialogue box so you can learn more.

Get insights into the dilemma. Look at their view of the problem. You might ask, "What is making this a problem?" Ask what they would like to see happen. You want to hear their truths and work with their truths. When VJ immediately rerouted our conversation to his defense of the manager, he was letting me know he was not interested in what I had to say. He unproductively changed the course of the conversation from listening to advising, directing and informing.

In contrast, Mensch HR people hold the person in front of them in high regard. They acknowledge the needs, perceptions, thoughts and position of the person in front of them. They also never act as if they know more than the person in front of them. They listen because they know there is more for them to learn. They recognize the constraints, frustrations or obstacles of the person in front of them. They abstain from evaluating, attacking, or judging.

Had I been in the job position to help people in the company be Mensches when communicating, I would have put an emphasis on being dialogical using good listening skills.

Listening opens up our field of awareness. It encourages us to put our opinions on the line and ask if they are accurate or useful. When we fully listen, we let go of the way we think things are supposed to be. Our world gets bigger when we pay attention to the speaker.

Whether you are in HR or management, when someone comes to you with their issue, the first thing you want to do is quiet your mind. Open the necessary space inside you to listen fully and take in what the person in front of you is saying. Make a commitment to completely surrender to the person who is speaking and listen fully. Be quiet more than 90% of the time. Speak to ask a question for clarity or to make comments that encourage the speaker to continue.

Use active listening skills to be sure you are hearing the message the speaker is sending. This will give you a better grasp of the speaker's needs, position and situation. It will pull you away from your making assumptions and leaping to conclusions. To listen effectively-and respectfully, apply these three techniques.

Mirror: Send back to the speaker what s/he said. Mimic the content of the communication. Simply repeat what is said saying words only and not feelings. Make sure you are correct in what you heard. Then ask if they want to tell you more. Your questions may be something like, "What I heard you say was…" "Is that correct?" "Is there more?" Use their words and share what you notice.

Validate: Let the sender know you get the message sent and it makes sense. It is an acknowledgement that the sender's experience has its own reality and validity. You might say, "It makes sense that when you chose not to accept me as a friend on Facebook it was because…" Reframe by putting the other person's meaning into your own words. This takes more thought than mirroring and also creates more awareness.

Empathize: Reflect, identify and capture the feeling (not the thought) of the speaker's message. Your comment may resemble this: "I imagine you feel sad or discouraged or rejected when you experienced…" Paraphrase and reflect back the person's description or feelings about the situation.

Summarize key points and always ask speaker if you are hearing message correctly. Report observations objectively. Track the conversation and pay attention to your own reactions. If you find yourself giving an opinion or making a judgment, catch yourself and change paths to objectivity.

Ask more than tell. Ask to explore. Use open ended questions such as "What do you think could be going on?" or "What might be some other things contributing to this?" or "What do you think would help turn this situation around?" or "How do you think we should address this?"

Probe further by making comments such as "tell me more about it" or "please elaborate further" or "help me understand better."

Do not add your opinion or judgement. Reflect what you see and hear. When you do, you not only show your interest but also your openness and objectivity.

We need new conversations in the workplace. We need to show compassion and caring when we converse.

Chapter **14**

The Human Side of the Organization

Hiring and Promoting

STEVE JOBS ATTRIBUTED much of the success of Apple Inc. to hiring the best. He hired A+ players. The number one job leaders have is to ensure capable people are working in the organization. Hire people who know tons of stuff you haven't even imagined. To hire people at least as smart as you (or hopefully smarter) in areas in which you do not excel, you need to have self-assurance and an appreciation of your own unique gifts.

Non Mensch people fear being shown their inadequacies so prefer to surround themselves with those whose intelligence and skill set are at a lower level. A Non Mensch leader often ignores his/her own insecurities that affect work. Yet this lack of knowledge can be destructive. Your insecurities and faults become much more discernable to others the more you don't recognize, acknowledge, and work with both. If you don't like the idea of surrounding yourself with ambitious, passionate, bright, and self-motivated achievers, you have to do a deep dive into yourself and discover the root cause and then find strategies to transform your attitude. Non Mensch leaders more often hire and promote those who are their sycophants or 'brown nosers.' I personally call these Stepford employees (my apologies to Ira Levin).

Mensch leaders are secure enough to not be threatened by others' talents and expertise. They know their own success is because of the smart, talented people working with them. They are comfortable to step aside and let others the chance to lead the way. They are willing to learn from others. [adapted from Jeff Rich when CEO of ACS]

A Mensch leader knows to weave together the great individual talents and the diversity of skills and strengths of staff members to create a significant whole. A Mensch has enough humility to recognize his/her own limitations and is not weighed down by pride to ask for help.

Employees expect you to have a hiring and promoting process that matches individual's talents, skills, experience and education with job requirements.

While the company policy for the company in my lawsuit mentioned that employment decisions are based solely upon an individual's qualifications relating to the requirements of the position for which the individual is being considered, it seemed for me senior leadership neither ignored their pre-conceived notions nor eliminated cognitive bias. Individuals were continually offered new positions, new job functions, and new job titles. There was not a characteristic or quality that ran unilaterally among these people. Changes and promotions were given to men and women, all generations, blond as well as brunette, tall and short. It was only the Jewish person who did not get any changes.

Employee growth and evolution

"If you want one year of prosperity, grow grain. If you want ten years of prosperity, grow trees. If you want one hundred years of prosperity, grow people." –A Chinese Proverb

Mensch leaders move people to be more than they imagined they ever could be. They trust and motivate the employees to be empowered to take risks that allow them to perform above levels with which they have become comfortable.

An educated, learned staff offers a competitive edge sustainable over time.

> **"Employee training and development is not an episodic event; it's an ongoing daily process."**
> -Myrtle Potter, Genentech, Inc.'s COO.

It is for this reason I suggested to move me from training on the product we supplied to subscribers to providing leadership education for the upwardly mobile. I was well equipped with knowledge and experience to provide valuable resources, tools and strategies for all staff to build skill sets and to take powerful action.

Mensch leaders encourage employees to identify, nurture and trust their talents and to try new things. They capture, cultivate and capitalize on the strengths of the people. Organizations need to recognize the hierarchy of performers per their skills, education, experience and knowledge. Then they need to treat people accordingly. It may seem counter intuitive but it is true that employees should not be treated equally. Each has his/her own unique talents, skills, experiences and qualifications as well as level of competency and intelligence.

Mensch companies ensure each employee is provided opportunities for accomplishment and pursuit of their passions. Mensch leaders know their responsibility is to help employees grow and develop to continually take on new and stronger responsibilities. They welcome to the organization those who want to be pushed to become better tomorrow than they were yesterday.

Non Mensch organizations fail to let people grow and aspire to their highest good. They keep their employees 'boxed up' and keep them all the same.

Job assignments need to be challenging. When the manager, HB, focused my reviews on minutia and gave me the lowest score on those menial tasks, she did not take personal responsibility for giving these tasks to the wrong person. If managers are not ready to assign projects that are in line with the unique experiences, qualifications, skills, and talents of the people in their department, they shouldn't be managers.

On occasion we were asked to divulge our own assessment of our performance at the company. I wrote in response for areas in which I can improve, "Currently I am content and fulfilled with my performance level." On another self-evaluation for the same question I wrote, "If I improved, it would be icing on the cake." This was not an attempt at being arrogant and haughty but rather realistic. My commenting on not needing to improve became a topic of question and answer in my deposition.

Defense asked, "So you don't believe in the philosophy there's always room for improvement?" I answered that in life I definitely believe in continuous improvement. I just didn't see a reason or need to improve at my job. The company should not have been surprised that I felt no need to improve. When work becomes boring and lacks purpose, it is common and typical for employees to check out.

Daniel Yankelovich, a public opinion analyst and social scientist as well as an author of many books on the workplace, coined the term "discretionary effort." He describes discretionary effort as the difference between the maximum amount of effort and care an individual can contribute and the minimum amount necessary to avoid being punished or fired. Each employee can contribute or withhold as s/he chooses.

When I saw they hired and maintained substandard skilled people in management positions, I saw no need to improve nor had a desire to do so. For me, improving would be analogous to moving the deck chairs on the sinking Titanic.

A business grows to the level of its employees' competencies, motivation, and output. It is then the responsibility of management, senior and otherwise, to create an environment that encourages continuous improvement and rewards such. Companies that have an environment that pushes hard working, highly skilled, respected, dedicated and sincere people to the point where they no longer care, will have a staff who find no need to do more than the minimum required. It is important for those in leadership roles to tap into the desires, abilities, and intrinsic motivations of the employees.

As an employee, form alliances with colleagues and superiors who encourage your best efforts and challenge you to grow. Stay away from Non Mensch managers and leaders who are mostly concerned with their self-promotion or lead from their insecurities.

Keep the best, let go of the rest.

The one expert skill a leader can never do without is recognizing smart and motivated people and giving them the autonomy to do their jobs in their area, and then rewarding them accordingly. Good people develop best ideas and generate most creative action plans. They implement those plans better than anybody else.

Reward only the very best. They are very marketable and the first to update résumés when unhappy. When employees get the best information, they exercise their sound judgment and will do their best to get measurable results. When good people leave, they take their knowledge, experience and contacts with them.

Turnover is mostly a manager issue that better pay, perks and training cannot remedy. People have a bigger need to be treated well and valued highly than they do for money. When I asked the CEO, CM, to change my job title and responsibilities, I specifically told him I was not looking for an increase in pay. Employees want to work in an environment in which they are appreciated and treated with dignity and respect. Best employees go first because they have the most options.

Companies and managers must understand what they do that contributes to the attrition of star employees. Retain talented employees by providing opportunities to grow and develop, as well as give substantiated reasons to continuously improve. High performers need to be properly acknowledged with greatest rewards and chronic poor performers finally need to be removed. If poor performers leave, the organization can benefit. If they don't leave, good people will leave and the organization will suffer. Most exiting employees state they will miss their co-workers more than anything else.

Acknowledge that talented people today have many other options. Financial reward is not enough. If you want them to work productively for you, your work environment has to be a place in which they can take real ownership.

Mensch management-it's the only way to have management

The central relationship between manager and employee is the most important and plays a critical role. It is the immediate manager who is responsible for motivating and engaging staff as much as they are responsible for impeding productive behavior in their employees. When senior leadership finds a chronically high level of employee disengagement (uncommitted), they need to assess the competency of their managers rather than badger the employees. They must lead managers in the direction of building relationships with employees to achieve significant productivity gains.

Management is complex mostly because it deals with people and people are complex. Every person in a management position should be able to illustrate how their efforts to humanly and compassionately get people around them to achieve more than they ever thought possible. Managers need to deliver tangible and practical results. Good managers must familiarize themselves with the different behavior styles of people and understand how their motivations and fears impact individual and collective performance.

Mensch leaders continually learn what their people need in order to do their best work.

Organizations need to continually assess a manager's capacity. Besides getting performance reviews from their managers, all those in leadership positions should solicit feedback from their department staff on their repertoire of skills, attitudes and approaches. Whether it be a formal or informal assessment, managers should take this information and create a development action plan to improve. Then they need to be held accountable for implementation. The assessment needs to be done on a regular schedule-every 6-12 months. If the scores from their staff don't indicate there is a significant increase in the level of competence, the manager needs to be considered a bad fit for the position and should be either given another position or terminated.

> **"The single biggest decision you make in your job- bigger than all the rest-is who you name manager. When you name the right people to manage your company's workplace, everything goes well... When you name the wrong person manager, nothing fixes that bad decision. Not compensation, not benefits-nothing"**
>
> –Gallup CEO Jim Clifton.

People leave managers and not companies. Allegedly CM admitted to an employee who was leaving the company that the training manager, HB, was wrong for the position. Even if you do put the wrong person in a position, skills can be taught/learned and attitudes can be readjusted.

Employees count on you to place well qualified people in management positions. They expect you to have:

- 8-10 specific core competencies for each manager to meet

- Well defined management characteristics

- Standards or by-laws for management

- Minimum management skill non-negotiable requirements

At the company where I worked, performance evaluations went down the organizational chart. Just the same, there was much evidence that my manager was a poor choice. Just because a person is assigned a role, does not mean the person is good at it.

Within the first year of her employment as a manager, one team member left because of his irritation with her. In his resignation email to the CEO, RB, he stated, "it is she and not I who should have walked out the door." Over the next few years, a minimum of eight people left the department or the company claiming she was the number one reason. Complaints about her ran rampant. Our whole team of trainers met with the CEO, RB to discuss her inadequacies. Others went individually to the CEO to discuss their concerns. In her deposition, the HR Director truthfully said that in their exit interviews, employees ridiculed her management style. One employee went as far as to say in her deposition that this manager's function was food and beverage. And nothing was ever done.

It should have been enough when 9 people left the company or department stating the incompetence of this same manager. It should have been enough when the entire team went to speak with the then CEO to describe this manager's lack of skill sets to manage effectively. It should have been enough when several individuals spoke with leadership about her. It should have been enough when the CEO, RB, told her that the new staff person, CM would not report to her. It should have been enough when CEO, RB told an employee he recruited from his previous job that he did not want her to report to this manager. It should have been enough when the HR Director heard during exit interviews stories pointing out this manager's inabilities. And it certainly should have been enough when the manager told me I was dead because I did not reveal Jesus to me.

I was once told: If one person calls you a horse's ass, ignore it; if two people call you a horse's ass, consider it; if three people call you a horse's ass, buy yourself a saddle.

Allowing poor managers to linger after 3+ incidences of deplorable management represents a failure of senior leadership. It is senior leadership then and not the employees who need to take responsibility for the manager's actions and pay the consequences. Once you continue to ignore the bad behaviors of a manager, you lose the privilege of condemning the employee.

Respect-it's what we all want

I was brilliantly taught by my manager at a fortune 100 company, 'you need to respect the position but you don't need to respect the person.' I lived by that in my future employment. Upper management at my last company was unaware of the power of the statement. No person, no matter what his/her position, can force anyone to respect another person-yes, respect their position in the organization, but not necessarily the person. Individual respect is earned. If upper management is insistent on having each employee respect each manager as a person, then the onus is on the organization to have a system in place that assists managers in becoming respect worthy.

It is respect for the person and not the position that makes one accept feedback given. When the topic about the anonymous letter that allegedly a subscriber sent to my manager describing his/her criticism of me, defense questioned me about feedback. I initially stated that when I get feedback, no matter from whom, I take what works for me and throw away the rest. He followed that with his question, "so if HB gives you feedback and you don't think it works for you, you don't follow it, right?" I advised him by summarizing much of what I have learned about feedback. Feedback is usually from the person's experiences. So when I coach people on feedback, I let them know what you hear may not be the absolute truth. It is being spoken from the speaker's view of the world. That view may not be part of my value system. I don't expect anyone to always act on the feedback someone offers. We are who we are and no one has the right or privilege to change us. If their feedback makes us stretch too much or we don't feel comfortable making the change, we don't have to. I am not talking about insubordination or rejecting directives that would be disrespectful of the manager's position. I am talking about when the person speaks straight from their values. Many times the feedback is valid and productive. If so, then accept it.

Still referencing the anonymous letter, defense added, "So you disregard any suggestions or tips HB provided you." "No," I replied. "I did not say I would disregard any". Key word here is 'any.' Even if I were given proof it was a subscriber who wrote the letter, the manager offered me no suggestions that I did not know already or had not used in previous times. I also did not respect her level of intelligence and no one can make anyone respect that.

You probably heard this before: good leaders lead by example and model the behavior they expect of others. Since wiser people than I have initially made this claim, I suggest that those who want to have an organization where managers are respected for who they are, they themselves treat each staff member with total respect. Sometimes to acknowledge and show you have respect for somebody else, you need to downplay your persona and get into theirs. Respect is quite contagious and by demonstrating how it is done can save much time and money in other forms of training. Once a manager shows a lack of respect for the people in her department, she loses the privilege of getting respect. Earn people's respect and you earn their loyalty.

Respecting the position means an employee does not commit insubordination which would be a high level of defiance or unruliness. It also does not mean one should be docile or meek or that one cannot disagree with any manager.

During a department meeting the manager verbally behaved abusively to everybody present. She wouldn't listen to anyone. I was saying something benign and productive to which she responded that maybe I want to be defensive and start yelling back. The discussion between my manager, HB, and me began to heat up. I observed her defensive behavior to unfold and I was sure an argument was making headway. I didn't want that to happen so I said to her (as phrased in the deposition) "hold off saying something to me until you can control yourself and not be defensive." Defense attorney asked, "Is that a way to speak to your manager?"

It is a way to speak to anyone if it subverts a bad situation. Titles are not entitlements to disorderly behavior.

It is not about being a manager but about being a human being and humanness surpasses one's placement on the organizational chart. Just because the manager does not know how to subvert a strong conflict, doesn't mean someone who does should remain silent.

Heightened anger is no place to discuss issues.

When conflicts become an issue, I always tell my coaching clients to hit the pause button. "Take a break," I tell them. "Cool down and only come back when you are calm." It is not always both people who simultaneously know to take a break. When either party realizes the argument is taking control over the people, that person has the responsibility to suggest a rest period to sooth oneself and get to a calmer state. I then proceed to give them an exercise to relax.

- Remove yourself from the place where the argument is brewing

- Sit in a comfortable chair

- Close your eyes and take a few deep breaths

- Imagine a place for you that you associate calmness and tranquility. Imagine being there. Focus on the pleasant feelings you are experiencing

- Concentrate on releasing all the tension that was building up

- Keep breathing slowly and deeply

- Once you feel calmed and know you can leave your 'fight' mode, return to discussion of the issue

I was not asking my manager to do anything I would not expect from anyone else with whom I have contact. Being a manager does not exempt one from receiving productive and solid advice. Taking a time out is a great way to start normalizing feelings.

I was interrogated in my deposition about my not going to the HR

Director to complain about the holiday party I found discomforting. Defense attorney was relentless in his inquiry and after accusing me of having no intentions of telling the HR Director about my reaction to the party stated, "Why would you have waited a few days to do it (go to HR) if you were going to complain? After speaking with HB, why didn't you go talk to HR person then, at that point?"

There is nothing wrong with letting our emotions and a situation simmer. I actually call this letting things percolate giving us space and time to think things through so we are not reactive. Never is it out of line to 'complain' after consideration, fact finding or just 'cooling off.' Letting it percolate does the following:

- Diffuses steam often resulting in our seeing the issue as no longer important

- Allows us to speak from a place of intellect and not emotion

- Gives us an opportunity to focus on something requiring more of our attention

When there is a conflict, there are two things we can do: fuel it so it festers and explodes (hitting rock bottom) or stepping up to the plate and changing the course of the conflict to a conversation.

People in conflict often focus their attention on blaming and attacking each other or each other's ideas. When doing so the discussion never moves to the deeper levels of understanding required to transform the conflict. We often stay in conflict because holding our position seems to give us a false sense of power and control. We avoid conversation because every honest conversation poses a risk that we will hear something that undermines our assumptions or changes us forever. Yet it is conversations that can lead to our having shifts in thinking, feeling and acting. Conversations can create an opening for learning, growth, and improvement. Quality of relationships is in conversations. Everything happens through conversations.

Confrontation should not be banned or punished. In a confrontational setting both parties need to access their respectable behaviors. The key is for all staff to be trained in the skills that will make confrontation with dignity acceptable and expected.

I follow the teachings of John Gottman, a famous psychological researcher and clinician, who says that how you start the conversation paves the way for the rest of the conversation because it sets the tone, pace, and attitude. He suggests using a soft start up as opposed to a harsh start up. A harsh start up (like 'why did you…?' or 'you always…') makes the other person feel attacked. Their first priority then is to protect themselves and they often do this by being defensive. It is difficult to feel attacked and listen at same time. Usually blame, accusations, threats, orders and put-downs follow all of which aim to make the other person feel guilty.

A soft start up is not accusatory or sarcastic. It gives the issue to the speaker. Usually the conversation starts with statements such as, "I feel that when you…" or "How it looks to me is…" or "How I interpret that is….." or "What I saw, heard, felt was…" Then stay focused on the subject and talk about one issue at a time.

Discussions that lead off with criticism and/or sarcasm (form of contempt) will inevitably end negatively and probably without resolution of the problem. It is best to stop, take a breather and start over. Search for common ground and not conflict.

No employee should be condemned for reasonably diverting an argument or for offering a suggestion on how to better talk to him/her and no employee should ever be labeled boorish because they refuse to put up with the insolent and brazen behavior of their manager in a team meeting.

And in Conclusion

Now that you are at the end of the book, I hope you received the messages that were intended to be given.

For every senior leader in an organization:

Listen to your people and always allow them to speak. Never silence them. If you are ever confronted with an issue of discrimination or harassment or bias, nip it in the bud. If it becomes a charge with the EEOC, use that as a strong wakeup call and do everything possible to come to an acceptable agreement. Never, ever let it get to litigation. At any point, build a bridge and move from adversarial to collaborative with the employee. Be sure your managers are the right people with that title. Train them accordingly and if they cannot be good managers, remove them from the position. If you don't, be prepared to take on the consequences without putting the burden on the employees. Be sure to set aside your ego and prejudices and look at the bigger picture when making employment decisions.

For every executive leader of a Board of Directors:

When you are advised of a lawsuit, ask many questions and do an investigation. If the plaintiff asks to meet with you, be sure you do so. Never abdicate any responsibility you have. You are also liable for discrimination. Question the credibility of a CEO who makes extremely important decisions without your input or at minimum input from anyone else.

For every individual:

If you are someone who thinks you have been treated unfairly, whether it is legally considered discrimination or not, speak up. Never remain silent. If you are involved in the legal process, be aware that the opposing attorney will play any games and tricks to confuse and mislead you. Stay focused.

Know that you are allowed to be treated with respect and dignity. Others do not have permission to treat you any way you don't want to be treated. When others judge you for your values or beliefs, they are engaging in bullying and that behavior is unacceptable. Don't take it-let them know they need to change their behaviors with you.

Know that you have the ability to make contributions and a real difference in every situation by bringing your full presence into the situation. Learn to value yourself and your contributions. Each of us needs to continually do a deep dive into ourselves to make repairs necessary. It is only then we can take on the responsibility given to each of us to make this a better world.

And the only way we can make it a better world is for each of us to always choose to be a Mensch.

Marcy Rich is available to speak and train on many areas of bettering ourselves as human beings. Please contact her if she can help at your:

Churches or Synagogues, Associations, schools, meet-ups, community groups, non-profit organizations/clubs, civic organizations, municipalities, businesses, networking groups, and more.

Marcy Rich is available for Coaching if you want to raise the quality of your relationships with partners, coworkers, family, friends, clients, and of course yourself.

For more information:
www.marcyrich.com
bookmarcyrich@gmail.com